## ADVANCE PRAISE FOR SELF PUBLISHING FOR VIRGINS

*"Self Publishing for Virgins" is a fantastic self-help book, jam-packed with all the information you need to publish that book you always wanted to write. The inspiring and systematic approach immediately caught my attention, and now I'm writing that book I always wanted to write. I couldn't put the book down!"*

~Carol Dykterok, MBA

*"Peggy gave direction to my energy. I knew what I wanted to do, but was not sure how to get there. Her guidance moved me forward to achieve my goals."*

~Cheri Powell, author
*Seven Tips to Getting the Most out of the Camino de Santiago*

*"I went from believing I could publish, to knowing I could publish, and had fun."*

~Cathy Courson, Licensed Clinical Social Worker

## LIST OF ILLUSTRATIONS and TRADEMARKS

CreateSpace™ is a trademark of Amazon.

Bluebeam PDF Revu™ is a trademark of BlueBeam PDF Revu, LLC.

Microsoft Word™ is a registered trademark of Microsoft Corporation.

In Design CS5™ and Adobe Acrobat™ are registered trademarks of Adobe, Inc.

All screenshots are used with permission from CreateSpace.

*Use of screenshots is not to be construed as an endorsement for this book by CreateSpace or Amazon.com.*

*To Doug and Hela,*
*Keep on writing.*
*6/20/2011*

# SELF PUBLISHING

# FOR

# VIRGINS

*The first-time author's guide to self publishing using*
*CreateSpace and print-on-demand technology.*

**FIRST EDITION**

Peggy Barnes DeKay

**DARBY PRESS**

Louisville, Kentucky

# SELF PUBLISHING FOR VIRGINS

www.selfpublishingforvirgins.com

This book is manufactured in the United States of America.

Publisher:
**DARBY PRESS**
10409 Cady Cove Court
Louisville, Kentucky 40223
(502) 303-7926

Orders: lrdandpld@yahoo.com

Editions ISBN
Soft cover     9780983414407
PDF            9780983414414

DeKay, Peggy Barnes
        Self  Publishing for Virgins
        Includes bibliographical references, index and appendices

LCCN        2011925081

Edited by Susan Lindsey of Savvy Communication LLC
www.savvy-comm.com

Cover character and interior characters by Darby Hampton

Book cover design by
Dave Mattingly

**Bulk orders:**

Quantity discounts are available on bulk purchases of this book for educational and training purposes. Discounts are also available to organizations, schools, libraries, corporations and others. To learn more, contact lrdandpld@yahoo.com or call (502) 303-7926.

**How to contact the author:**

Peggy Barnes DeKay is a writer, author and publishing consultant. She speaks on the self publishing industry in a variety of venues and teaches workshops and seminars on how to self publish, e-books and book marketing and promotion.

To contact Ms. DeKay for a speaking engagement, interview or appearance, please email her at pdkpost@gmail.com or visit her Web site at www.peggydekay.com.

Information in the self-publishing industry changes daily. For special reports, self-publishing updates and the latest developments, visit www.peggydekay.com. Readers of this book are also encouraged to contact the author with comments and ideas for future editions.

*"With sixty staring me in the face, I have developed inflammation of the sentence structure and definite hardening of the paragraphs."*

~James Thurber

# CONTENTS

WARNING AND DISCLAIMER ..................... xvi

DEDICATION................................................ xvii

ACKNOWLEDGEMENT ............................. xix

INTRODUCTION ........................................... xxi

HOW TO USE THIS BOOK ........................ xxiv

## PART ONE

### 1 SELF PUBLISHING: An Overview .....3

Why CreateSpace?........................................ 3

The POD Revolution ...................................... 4

Why Self Publish?......................................... 5

What Type of Books Sell Best? .................... 10

### 2 BUSINESS OF SELF PUBLISHING....15

Top Reasons to be an Author ....................... 15

Who Should Self Publish? ............................ 16

The CreateSpace Solution............................ 21

Top Five Traits of Great POD ....................... 22

### 3 FINDING YOUR MARKET ..............25

The Author Platform ........................ 25

Growing a Platform ........................ 26

Who is Your Reader? ........................ 27

Finding Your Market ........................ 28

## 4 BOOK ANATOMY ........................ 31

Building Your Book ........................ 31

BTIC ........................ 31

Book Anatomy ........................ 34

Front Matter ........................ 35

Interior Cover Page ........................ 36

Timing ........................ 38

Handling Graphics ........................ 38

Back Matter ........................ 38

Choosing a Title ........................ 40

## 5 EDITING ........................ 45

The First Draft ........................ 45

The Second Draft ........................ 46

Hiring an Editor ........................ 49

## 6 TOOLS FOR PUBLISHING ..............53

Layout Tools ..................................... 53

## 7 COPYRIGHT AND FAIR USE...........59

Copyright 101 ................................... 59

Permissions ..................................... 62

Fair Use and Plagiarism.................... 63

Registering Copyright ....................... 64

Copyright Clearance Center ............. 66

## 8 GETTING THE NUMBERS ..............71

ISBN ................................................ 74

Publisher of Record ......................... 75

Starting a Publishing Company..................... 78

Library of Congress Number (LCCN)............ 79

Cataloging in Publication (CIP)..................... 83

OCLC-World Cat............................... 86

## PART TWO

## 9 INTERIOR LAYOUT .......................91

Publishing Software ......................... 92

Keys to Clean Interior Design ....................... 93

Typeface and Font Size ............................... 94

Photos and Illustrations............................... 96

Trim Size.................................................... 97

Headers and Footers .................................. 103

Section Breaks............................................ 104

**10 BOOK COVERS THAT RULE ....... 109**

Seven Rules to a Great Book Cover ........... 113

Creating a Compelling Back Cover ............. 114

Testimonials or Blurbs ............................... 115

Author Bio ................................................. 116

**11 PRE-PUBLICATION FILE ............ 121**

Pre-publication File ..................................... 121

PDF File Explained ..................................... 121

Converting Your Book File to PDF .............. 122

**12 USING CREATESPACE................ 125**

Preparing Your Word File............................ 125

Getting Started with CreateSpace............... 128

Assigning an ISBN ................................. 140

LCCN ................................................ 142

Interior Layout Page ............................ 143

CreateSpace Cover Templates.................. 144

Author's Bio ...................................... 146

BISAC Category .................................. 149

CreateSpace Landing Page ...................... 149

Expanded Distribution Channel ................ 150

Getting a Proof.................................. 151

CreateSpace Commissions ...................... 152

Pro Plan........................................... 153

## PART THREE

## 13 TAKE YOUR BOOK TO MARKET 157

Making the Money Work ........................ 157

The Golden Rules of POD ...................... 158

Media Kit Components............................. 161

Radio and Television ............................ 162

News Release 101 ................................ 165

Building your Media List......................... 166

Sample Press Release ............................. 167

Building Your Expert Status ........................ 169

Writing Articles ....................................... 170

Podcasting ............................................. 172

**14 MAKE THE MOST OF AMAZON 175**

Amazon Author Central.............................. 175

Sales Info Tab........................................ 179

Geographic Sales .................................... 179

Amazon Ranking...................................... 179

Tags .................................................... 181

Amazon Editorial Review ............................ 182

Amazon Customer Reviews......................... 182

Top Reviewers ........................................ 183

Listmania............................................... 185

Amazon Associate ................................... 185

Amazon Encore ....................................... 186

**15 MARKET TO LIBRARIES ............ 189**

Distributors............................................. 189

CIP and Quality Books................................ 190

Changing Market ......................................... 193

Library Reviews .......................................... 193

## 16 CREATE AN AUTHOR WEB SITE 197

Web Site Basics.......................................... 197

Hiring a Web Designer................................ 199

List Building ................................................ 202

E-store ........................................................ 204

Sell through Amazon or DIY? ..................... 204

Resources................................................... 205

Web Site Sales Techniques........................ 206

## 17 USING SOCIAL MEDIA ..............209

Facebook .................................................... 210

aWeber ....................................................... 212

Twitter ......................................................... 212

LinkedIn ...................................................... 214

Specialty Sites for Authors......................... 215

## 18 MARKET WITH IMAGINATION..221

Independent Book Awards ........................... 223

Podcasts ................................................ 226

Retail Markets ........................................ 227

Selling to Indie Book Stores ..................... 228

Blogging ................................................ 229

FeedBlitz.com ......................................... 230

Feedburner.com ...................................... 231

Book Fairs .............................................. 233

Reviews ................................................. 235

## 19 CAREER BUILDING ................... 241

Building Intellectual Capital ...................... 241

Speaking for Dollars ................................ 242

Writing Articles ....................................... 244

Marketing to Associations ......................... 244

## 20 PUT IT ALL TOGETHER ............. 249

The Master Plan ...................................... 249

The Publisher's Calendar .......................... 249

Branding ................................................ 250

BIBLIOGRAPHY ............................... 252

APPENDIX A .................................... 253

APPENDIX B .................................... 257

GLOSSARY ...................................... 264

ABOUT THE AUTHOR ..................... 272

FORTHCOMING BOOKS ........................... 274

## WARNING AND DISCLAIMER

Although the author and publisher have exhaustively researched all sources used in this book to ensure the accuracy and completeness of the information contained herein, we assume no responsibility for errors, inaccuracies, omissions or any other inconsistencies. Any slights against people or organizations are not intentional. The information in this book is offered with the understanding that it does not contain financial, legal or other professional advice. If you have need of such services, you should consult with a competent professional.

The author and publisher make no claims as to the suitability of the information contained herein. The information is provided "as is" and without warranty of any kind. Neither the author nor the publisher shall be liable for damages arising here from. Citations of organizations and/or Web sites are not to be construed as an endorsement for said source or Web site.

This book may not contain all of the information that you are looking for on a given subject. The author has listed resource pages at the end of this book for your review that may be helpful to you.

While every attempt has been made to have the most current information available, technology changes quickly and some Web sites and other specific information may have changed.

Screenshots used in this book do not represent an endorsement of this book by Amazon or Createspace.com.

## DEDICATION

To Larry, Darby, Scott and Alex—*through much activity, a dream is accomplished.*

To Emma and Adeline Grace—all things are possible.

# ACKNOWLEDGEMENT

*Self Publishing for Virgins* is dedicated to the many would-be authors who want their voices heard. With the latest technology, and the freedom of a vibrant print-on-demand (POD) industry, this is more possible now than at any time in history.

I would like to thank and acknowledge the women of Women Who Write, Inc. (www.womenwhowrite.com) who helped me begin the journey. I want to thank Cathy Courson who read the book and gave me great suggestions. I also want to thank Peggy Grimes who embraced the concept of self publishing, and Emily Boone who teaches me daily that there is nothing I can't do. Together, they gave me strength to keep going.

Cheri Powell and Deanna O'Daniel who both came out with self-published books in 2010, are an ongoing inspiration to me. I want to thank Beth Wells who allowed me to think out loud. If she got tired of hearing about "the book" she never said so.

To my sons, Scott and Alex, I am grateful for their never wavering faith in me. I thank my sister, Barbara—thank you for believing in me one more time. I want to acknowledge my brother, Jerry, who didn't do a darn thing for this project, but has seen me through on so many in the past.

I want to thank my editor, Susan Lindsey, who is skilled and brave enough to tell me like it is without compromise. She helped to make this a better book for all of us.

I owe a great debt to my husband Larry who never complained, at least not for any length of time. He pushed me to completion even when it infuriated me. He has been my champion throughout this process and in my life. He is my everyday hero—but that's another book.

I want to thank my daughter, Darby, for creating the lovable cover character; she teaches me every day that marching to your own drummer is not just an idea, but a way of living.

This book is the fulfillment of a dream for me, and I hope in some way it will play a part in helping your dream of writing a book to come true. Here's to all of you, who dream of writing a book—someday—may all your dreams, and your books come to pass.

**MY MISSION**

Publishing this book was a defining moment in my life. What has happened to me can happen to you. You can become a published author. Will it be easy? No. Will it take a lot of hard work? Yes. But can it happen? Absolutely!

My mission is to teach writers how to create a professional, well-edited, self-published book that generates a profit for the author, is sold on Amazon.com and in bookstores, and gives the readers something of value—a great book. *If self publishing is your mission, then this book is your mentor!*

# INTRODUCTION

Three-hundred years ago a family might own only one book. It was usually a book called the *Book of Hours*. The *Book of Hours* was a family devotional and it was an expensive and prized family possession, handed down from generation to generation.

In those days, books were small, fitting easily in the palm of a hand. The text was painstakingly hand copied by a calligrapher or "scribe" onto whisper thin sheets of animal skins. The scribe could produce one or two books a year.

The animal skins were then sandwiched between two covers made of quarter-inch thick pieces of hard wood that measured approximately five by four inches. The pages were then stitched together at the binding and attached to the wooden covers. This is where the term "hard cover" originated.

Fast forward to today and we see that publishing has changed dramatically! Today an author with a completed manuscript, layout and cover design can take a book from the PC to a sales page on Amazon.com in a matter of days.

Although authors can now write, produce and market their books in months rather than years, the success of any book is still dependent on the quality of the book itself. If the book is not fun to read, intriguing, or solves a problem for the reader, chances are, no one will buy it or read it.

In a publishing world where only a well-established writer, an actor, a politician or an athlete can get a lucrative publishing contract from a traditional publishing house, the era of the self-published author is long overdue. Make no mistake, to have a successful book, and that means a book that people buy, hopefully in obscenely large numbers, it must still be a good read. My goal in writing *Self Publishing for Virgins* is to guide you, the first-time, self-published author through the seven stages of self publishing.

### Part One: Before Your Book is published

1. Understand the benefits of print-on-demand technology, and book pricing.
2. Learn about book anatomy, copyright and fair use.
3. Discover the importance of good editing and learn how to get an ISBN and LCCN.

### Part Two: Publishing Your Book

4. Lay out your book's interior using Microsoft Word 2007.
5. Learn how to create a PDF file.
6. Publish your book and sell it on Amazon and in bookstores with CreateSpace.

### Part Three: Post Publication Promotion

7. Make the most of Amazon and promote your book using social media and stealth marketing on a budget.

If your book is already written, then you are starting this book on step four or five. The remaining steps can be completed or put into motion in 30 days. If you have not yet written your book, but know what you want to write about, you need to do some market research. The process can take time, but if you are committed to writing your book, you can finish in a *season*. If you bought this book to research self publishing, then you are at step one and the process from start to finish may take longer.

*Costs*

Since most self-published authors operate on a tight budget, I have deliberately chosen software that is popular, perhaps already installed on your PC and inexpensive.  When given the option of using expensive applications or inexpensive ones, I chose the more affordable ones that did not compromise functionality.

I have tested my choices to use CreateSpace, Word and BlueBeam. I have used all of these applications, and I know they work. One last reminder: your book, whether self-published, or published by a traditional publisher, is destined to become a part of your body of work. Make it count. Produce a professional work because in the age of the Internet, once your book is published and posted for sale on public sites like Amazon.com and others, it will be out there for many years to come.

# HOW TO USE THIS BOOK

## Part One: Before Publication

This book is written in three parts. Part One provides an overview of self-publishing and covers the first three steps in publishing your book. It explains why self publishing using print-on-demand has and will continue to take the publishing world by storm. You will learn about copyright and fair use, and how to set a sell price for your book. You will learn how to register your book with national databases that are vital to selling your book online and in bookstores. You will learn why, how, and when to acquire an Industry Standard Book Number (ISBN) and Library of Congress number (LCCN or LCN).

In Part One and throughout this book, I try to help you avoid mistakes. Early decisions can impact your ability to sell your book in certain markets. They can affect both long-and short-term sales, where your book is listed, and how accessible it is to huge markets.

## Part Two: Getting Your Book Published

Part Two looks at the process of designing a book. In Part Two, we cover interior book layout and cover design. You will learn how to create a PDF file for uploading to your POD printer. Part Two will show you how to set up your author account with CreateSpace and physically prepare and publish your book. You will learn how to list your book for sale on Amazon and CreateSpace. In Part Two, you will learn how to take advantage of CreateSpace's Expanded Channel distribution network for selling your book in bookstores and in other markets.

## Part Three:

## Reaching Your Reader

In Part Three, you will learn how to successfully promote and market your book. You will learn how to reach your reader in both traditional and non-traditional ways. Next we look at author Web sites and what makes a successful writer's Web site. We will cover writing an effective press release and, more importantly, when to write one. In Part Three, you will learn the basic components of a media kit, and how to promote your book using social media like Facebook, Twitter and LinkedIn.

You will also learn how to make the most of Amazon and Amazon's author account. You will learn how Amazon ranks books and how to monitor sales of your book compared to other books in your genre. In Part Three, you will learn about stealth marketing, and how authors can promote their books in non-traditional ways without spending a fortune.

### Finding Your Starting Point

This book is written in three parts for a reason. I want this book to be helpful to first-time, self-published authors. But not all first-time, self-published authors are at the same place in their writing careers. For some of you, this is your first book, self-published or otherwise; for some, your book is written and you want the nuts and bolts of getting your book published; and for some, you simply want inventive ways to market your book.

That means that beginners will start in Part One; those with completed books will spend most of their time in parts two and three. Those of you who have already dabbled in self publishing will spend most of your time in Part Three.

### *Virgin's Notes*

The *Virgin's Notes*, in Part One, are for new authors. They give you practical advice and real life stories from authors who have been where you are going.

### *Author's Notes*

Author's Notes, which appear in Part Two, give you advice and stories geared to the successful publication of your book.

### *Marketer's Notes*

Marketer's Notes, in Part Three, give you inside information about marketing and promoting your book.

### *Self Publisher's Checklist*

The self publisher's checklist is found at the end of each chapter. Use these lists to build your publisher's calendar.

# PART ONE

# WHAT YOU WILL LEARN IN THIS CHAPTER

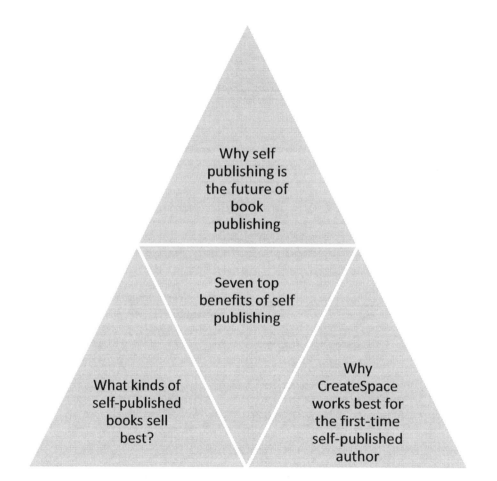

# 1 SELF PUBLISHING: An Overview

*"The Web site [Amazon] is designed to help customers find books they didn't know existed."* ~Greg Greeley, Amazon VP Media Products

## Success Stories

It's 4 p.m. and you hear a knock at your door, then the sound of steps walking away. You rush to the door and peek out, but see no one. Cautiously, you open the door to reveal an empty porch, except for a large, cardboard envelope. You pick up the envelope, rush inside and shut the door behind you. *Can it be—the object you have been waiting for is finally here?* You tear open the package and remove a beautiful perfect bound book. The cover is slick and glossy, covered with brilliant colors and the title is perfect (if you do say so yourself). Then you see it, at the bottom of the front cover under "By" is a name you recognize. *Yours!* Finally, what was once only a dream has become a reality, your reality. Now what seemed available to only the famous and privileged has come to you. *You are a published author!*

## Why CreateSpace?

In this book, we will be using CreateSpace and print-on-demand (POD) technology to self publish your book. I chose CreateSpace based on the following criteria: *best functionality combined with ease of use, offered at the lowest price.* My second consideration was the connection between

Amazon.com and CreateSpace, which is a division of Amazon. This means that the integration between publishing with CreateSpace and listing your book for sale on Amazon is seamless—a significant advantage for the first-time, self-published author. I don't get paid by CreateSpace or Amazon to say that. I have used CreateSpace to produce other books and I truly believe that they are the best fit for the first-time, self-published author.

### Virgin's Note

*This year, author Raymond Bean self published a book about a boy who is accused of stinking up his school. The book is called* Sweet Farts. *As his book rose in the Amazon rankings, it got the attention of two Asian publishers who offered him a deal, which prompted Amazon Encore to give him a sweeter deal! This is great news for Mr. Bean, but it is also great news for you. When you have a successful book that is selling a lot of copies, it will get noticed, people will buy it, and the fact that it is self published won't matter.*

## The POD Revolution

Do you remember a few years ago when the Japanese came up with an inventory concept called "just-in-time inventory?" It was all the rage in business books and still is today. The rationale of just-in-time inventory is that businesses can lower costs by keeping inventory levels as low as possible, then ordering new inventory just in time to fill the incoming orders.

POD works the same way. Authors who self publish don't have to buy 500 or 1,000 books upfront and store them in their garage. If you are looking at POD companies now, and they are requesting an upfront, minimum order of 500 or more books—walk away.

As a self-published author using CreateSpace, there is no minimum purchase required and your book will automatically be listed for sale on Amazon.com.

## Why Self Publish?

A better question is, "Why NOT self publish?"  The author who has his or her book published by a traditional publisher will make, on average, between one and two dollars in royalties per book sold. A self-published author can make three to eight times more profit per sale, depending on the circumstances of the sale. You can make more money while retaining creative control.

## Seven Key Benefits of Self Publishing

1. **Bigger Profits** - Traditional publishers pay you 10 to 12 percent royalties on each book sold. Self published authors can make, depending on the type of sales transaction, up to 80 percent!
2. **Creative control** - Your book is a reflection of who you are. With POD and self publishing, you have control over the creative process and its outcome—your book.
3. **You Own Your Book** - Traditional publishers buy the rights to your book; with self publishing you retain the rights, a key factor in self publishing.
4. **Shortened Time to Market** - Take your book to market in weeks instead of months or years with a traditional publisher.
5. **Guaranteed Publication** - You are no longer dependent on a traditional publishing industry that only wants to buy blockbuster books from celebrity authors.

6. **Entrepreneurialism** – You, as the author, are free to market your book in any way you see fit. With inexpensive author copies, you can sell your book anywhere, anytime, and make money.
7. **Legacy** - Your book is a part of your legacy. It is your mark on the world; your gift to those who love and believe in you.

### Virgin's Note

*Another great benefit of self publishing is that you can keep your book current and recover from errors more quickly with far less expense. When you have a typo in a traditionally published book, and it happens, you may have thousands of books already printed and stored in a warehouse. With self publishing, you can take your book "out of print" electronically, fix the typo, reload the publication file and "re-publish" your book. Temporarily taking your book out of print to make a correction means you don't have to live with the error until all of your books are sold.*

Many traditional publishers expect the author to pay for a book tour. If you have to spend your dollars on marketing, shouldn't you be getting the lion's share of the profits? With self publishing, you can.

Statistically, most self-published books are sold either online, through independent book stores or in non-traditional settings. As a self-published author, traditional book stores like Barnes & Noble are often the last place you will sell your book.

Here's the reality. Whether you publish your book with a traditional publisher or self publish, **you will still have to market your book**. You are going to be intricately involved in marketing your book anyway—so why not self publish? As the author, you are the best and most enthusiastic promoter of your book. No one will care about your book as much as you do.

Have you ever wondered why you continue to hear more and more buzz around POD and self publishing? Because it works! Authors have discovered the freedom, and the profitability that only self publishing can give them.

Dan Poynter, a self-published author who has written more than 120 books, is often called the godfather of self publishing. His first self-published book was about parachutes. It was rejected over and over again by traditional publishers because they felt the market for a book about parachutes wasn't large enough to sustain profitable sales. He decided to self publish his book instead and it became a prolific seller and is still selling today.

There are three factors that drive book sales in today's self-publishing environment—*speed, specialization and profit.*

## Speed, Specialization and Profit

Twenty years ago, the World Wide Web was new. People craved information, and while it was readily available on the Internet, most people didn't have access. To meet the growing need for information, books were written with all-encompassing titles like *"Everything You Will Ever Need to Know About …,"* or *"The Complete Guide to …."*

Fast forward to today. The information highway is now like the German Autobahn; if you can keep up, get on! With the proliferation of information and access, we now have a different problem—vast amounts of data at our fingertips that we have to sift through.

Enter the age of specialization. Today's readers are looking for specific information and have a narrow focus. They don't have time to sift through data irrelevant to their purpose. Have you been to the pet store lately? If you look at the magazine rack you will see a magazine for nearly every breed of dog or cat. Books are no different. This book, for example, is not just a book about how to self publish; it is a book about to self publish using CreateSpace. This is specialization and it works.

Modern readers, raised on immediate access to information of all types, want specific, subject-related information—*now*. This need has driven the dramatic rise of narrowly focused books or "niche" books.

As a self-published author, should you be excited about niche books? *Yes*. Here are a few examples of niche books that sold at least 50,000 copies.

| BOOK TITLE | NUMBER COPIES SOLD |
|---|---|
| Celtic Needlepoint | 50,000 |
| How to Live with a Neurotic Dog | 60,000 |
| Scrapbook Basics | 60,000 |
| From Panic to Power | 72,000 |
| Polish Your Furniture with Pantyhose | 85,000 |
| The Case of the Creator | 150,000 |
| Lawyers and Other Reptiles | 150,000 |
| Everyone Poops | 500,000 |
| South Beach Diet | 7,429,000 |
| The Prayer of Jabez | 9,000,000 |

**Figure 1.3**    Figures taken from Marc McCutcheon's book Dam*n! Why Didn't I Write That?*

Today there are 51 million iPhones/iPods/iPads; 100 million other smart phones; five million e-link devices and more than 30 million net book computers. All of these devices use and distribute information delivered to customers in books, print books and e-books.

Keep in mind that if a book is self published and done properly, the profit margin is much greater than the royalty payment paid through a traditional publisher. This means that book sales of 5,000 copies of a self-published book may yield as much profit to the author as three to five times the sales using a traditional publisher.

*There has never been a better time in the history of the world to be a self-published author.*

## What Type of Books Sell Best?

For every 180 books written and offered for sale each year, only 35 are works of fiction, or about one in five. Most books published today are non-fiction. These books and their huge sales numbers illustrate the power of the *niche non-fiction book*. Someone once said that to be successful in any business you must identify a need and then fill it. Niche book authors have successfully identified the needs and written the books that meet those needs.

## Famous Self Published Authors

Self publishing is an idea that has been around for a long time. Many authors, past and present, have self published with astounding success. Authors of the past such as Mark Twain, Gertrude Stein, Zane Grey and Carl Sandburg, and more recent authors like Deepak Chopra, Tom Clancy and Jack Canfield have all been unabashed, self-published authors.

If your self-published book is well done and has good sales, it will be noticed by traditional publishers.

Getting the attention of a traditional publisher can be a good thing—if you are smart about your contract. There are stories about successful self-published authors who have sold their books to a traditional publisher only to find that after a six-week flurry of advertising, the publisher does nothing more to promote their books. I have known authors who have had their books go out of print in six months after selling to a traditional publisher.

*Virgin's Note*

*Dan Miller, a prolific writer, life coach, consultant and podcaster (listen to Dan at 48days.com) tells a story about one of his books that was picked up by a traditional publisher. The publisher sold his book as part of a promotional package to a large retailer. Many of the books were not sold and were returned by the retailer to the publisher. Dan bought the returned, unsold books from the publisher for pennies on the dollar. He then sold the books on his Web site at steep discounts and made a great profit! This is just smart business. If your self-published book becomes popular, you may get offers from traditional publishers. If you do, make sure you can buy back returns cheaply. You also want to make sure that if the book goes out of print, that the rights to the book revert back to you, the author.*

If your book is a memoir, a mystery or a children's book, it can be self published. The key to a successful self-published book is not just the type of book. A quality book with high production standards, great writing and smart marketing will sell every time!

With CreateSpace you can take your completed manuscript from your PC to a sales page on Amazon in a week.

So, take some time when reading over the next few chapters and get the right mindset. Now is your time, if you choose to take advantage of it!

### *Virgin's Note*

*What is the overall trend for self-published books? We, as reading, book-buying consumers, are trending toward information and technology. The modern day reader wants to be better informed, better educated and more competitive in his or her field—and is willing to pay for it. What does this mean for you as a writer? You need to focus on solving a problem for your reader. Look for niche markets. It is better to write about an Anatolian Shepherd than to write a book about all breeds of dogs. Find a niche or a group of people who have a problem, determine what that problem is, and then write the book that solves the problem!*

### *Self Publisher's Checklist*

- ✓ *I know how POD works.*
- ✓ *Think about your book topic.*
- ✓ *Know you can be a self-published author.*

*"I love being a writer. What I can't stand is the paperwork."*

~Peter De Vries

# WHAT YOU WILL LEARN IN THIS CHAPTER

Seven reasons to become a self-published author

CreateSpace the first time author's solution

Types of self publishing

Five traits of a great POD

# 2 BUSINESS OF SELF PUBLISHING

*"You can't always get what you want … but if you try real hard, you get what you need."* ~The Rolling Stones

## Am I Ready to Self Publish?

Make no mistake, as a self-published author you are in business—your business! Writing and promoting your book are equally important.

To write and finish a book, you need to have a realistic expectation of the level of work required. If you are ready, writing and publishing your book will be one of the most rewarding things you have ever done.

## Top Reasons to be an Author

Writing a book can build your business, generate a speaking career and open up opportunities that you never dreamed of. Let's review the benefits of being a self-published author.

1. It positions you as an industry expert.
2. Being an author gives you credibility.
3. Your book will attract your target audience.
4. Your book sets you apart with an instantly recognizable brand.

5.  A successful book wins the attention of traditional publishers.
6.  Consistently win more, higher paying speaking gigs.
7.  Create multiple streams of income.

## Who Should Self Publish?

Nearly 80 percent of all people, when asked if they have a book inside them, answer *yes*. There is no longer any excuse to leave that book inside you. Now is the time to self publish your book.

## Who Can Benefit from Self Publishing?

**Professionals** - Doctors, lawyers, sales professionals, dentists, chiropractors, life coaches, academics, CEOs and other business professionals. (Books are outstanding career builders! If you are an expert in your field, a book is in your future.)

**Writers** - Journalists, poets, memoirists, fiction and non-fiction writers, traditionally published authors, bloggers, biographers, children's books writers.

**Hobbyists** - Genealogists, family historians, crafters.

Whether you are a business expert, a journalist, historian or children's book writer, writing and publishing your book is more possible now than at any other time in history.

## The Creed

Now that we have talked about the significant advantages of self publishing, let's talk about your responsibilities as a self-published author. If you can commit to the principles below, you can write and publish your book.

- *I know the subject matter of my book.*
- *I know my reader and how to reach them.*
- *I have thoroughly fact-checked my book.*
- *I have had my book professionally edited.*
- *I have given proper attribution.*
- *I have a professional interior layout.*
- *I have a great book cover.*
- *I am willing to do whatever it takes, for as long as it takes, to tell people about my book.*

Tony Robbins, the motivational speaker stated, "If you want a better answer, ask a better question." Questions are the windows of opportunity. Take a few minutes and ask yourself the following seven questions. Really think about your answers.

## Self-Published Author's Quiz

1. Am I enthusiastic about writing the book?
2. Do I have the experience in this area or access to experts who do?
3. Is this a subject that will interest others?
4. Is my topic focused and well organized?
5. Do I know who my reader is?
6. Can I reach my readers with traditional marketing techniques?
7. Is the market large enough?

Look at the first question. I hope you answered it yes.  Some years ago, when I started my computer company, an old friend and successful entrepreneur told me something I will never forget. He said, *"Hard work will take you 20 percent of the way, but enthusiasm will take you the other 80 percent!"*

Grab destiny by the horns, and make the decision that could change the quality of your life for the better, for the rest of your life. Become a published author.

## How POD Works

The real beauty of POD is that it gives you the best of both worlds. It offers you a nearly no-cost fulfillment (most shipping is paid by the customer) and a distribution model that is already in place.

Your cost per book with a black and white interior, and less than 300 pages, will be $3.15 per book if you are using CreateSpace . Many POD's will charge you more; don't do it.

*Never pay more than 25-30 percent of the list price of your book for printing.*

## Types of POD Printers

### Vanity Press

One indication of a vanity press is the requirement to purchase a large number of books "up front." This beginning inventory requirement could be as high as 500 to 5,000 books. Vanity presses often charge the author 50 percent or more of the retail price of the book to purchase *author copies*. No author, no matter how skilled a marketer, can survive that level of profit gouging by the publisher. Author copies are the books that you buy from the printer to resell to other people directly.

If you give training seminars or you are a speaker, you will want to sell your books in person. The books you sell in person to your customers are author copies. This is why it is important that your price to buy copies is no more than 30 percent of the retail price of your book.

Vanity presses charge top dollar for providing ancillary services such as editing, interior layout, cover design, blurbs, registrations and reviews.

Dan Poynter, the self-publishing guru, talks about one woman who paid $176 per book by the time she was finished working with a vanity press.

## Partnered Self Publishing

Partnered self publishing houses offer "cafeteria style" services to the author. The partnered approach works well for many authors who are not technically oriented and who want to concentrate on writing. They typically offer editing, interior layout, cover design, Web site, marketing packages, public relations (PR), and book reviews. These services can be bundled for cost savings, or purchased separately.

The cheapest way to self publish is do all or most of the work yourself. The savings must be weighed against your technical skills as a book designer, editor, and marketer. If you feel you are lacking in one or more of these areas, then a partnered solution is ideal. Before you contract with a POD publisher, read the fine print. Know what your rights are and what you are getting for your money.

CreateSpace is a partnered POD, with one main difference. CreateSpace will let you do it all yourself, or use their services cafeteria style. They don't dictate your book pricing (some PODs tell you what you can charge for your book). Ancillary services such as editing, book cover design and interior layout are reasonably priced.

One key advantage of using CreateSpace is their pricing for author copies. Your author price from CreateSpace for a perfect bound, 200-page black and white interior book, will be $3 to $4. This relatively low printing price gives you room to offer discounts to buyers or resellers of your book.

The second key advantage to using CreateSpace is their relationship with Amazon.com. CreateSpace is a division of Amazon, so listing your book on Amazon is a seamless operation.

## Independent Self Publishing

In this scenario, you are the contractor. You hire the book cover designer, editor, and interior layout person and you do all the paperwork.

Independent self publishing is the least expensive way to publish your book, but can be the most demanding. Lightning Source is a great POD to use if you want to go this route. Lightning Source is a division of Ingram Books, which is the largest book distributor in the U.S.

Lightning Source works primarily with traditional publishers. They will assume that you know what to do, what forms to fill out and when to do it. Lightning Source works with all of the major distributors and wholesalers and your book will be available internationally.

Using Lightning Source is the cheapest of the three, but the most technically difficult. It is not the best choice for a first-time author.

***Virgin's Note***

*Print-on-demand works best for books that are fewer than 500 pages. Because POD is a high-speed solution for printing books, larger books can experience problems with registration. Ideally, a POD book is from 48 to 300 pages in length.*

## The CreateSpace Solution

When your book is published using CreateSpace, you will be given two landing pages. A landing page is essentially a one-page Web site, usually used to purchase a specific item. One landing page or sales page will reside on the CreateSpace server and the other landing page is on the Amazon.com server. CreateSpace will send you the link to your book's sales page (landing page). Both pages are set up automatically by CreateSpace using the data that you entered to set up your original account. Your books can be purchased online at either site.

When a customer orders your book from Amazon or CreateSpace.com, those companies handle fulfillment. The customer pays the shipping at the point of sale, and all you do is wait for your check.

Amazon and CreateSpace expect to make money on the sale, as well. Amazon charges a 40 percent commission (based on the retail price of your book) on each book sale originating from their site. CreateSpace charges a 20 percent commission (based on the retail list price) if the book is sold from their landing page.

## Pricing

Let's take a look at what a typical book sale might look like. Pricing and commissions are based on data from December 2010

| Sold on CreateSpace | | Sold on Amazon | |
| --- | --- | --- | --- |
| Retail book price | $16.95 | Retail book price | $16.95 |
| Printing cost | (3.15) | Printing cost | (3.15) |
| Commission | (3.39) | Commission | (6.78) |
| **Gross Profit** | **$10.41** | **Gross Profit** | **$7.02** |

The tables above assume you have purchased the CreateSpace Pro Plan and that the book is sold for the retail price. That may not be the case in all scenarios. The customer is paying the shipping on both of these examples. If you are selling your books directly to an independent (indie) bookstore you may be paying the shipping, or you may have then drop-shipped to the bookstore. Either way, you are paying the shipping.

## Top Five Traits of a Great POD

1. You retain the rights to your work.
2. You are free to move your book elsewhere (provided you purchased your own ISBN).
3. Author copies cost less than 30 percent of the retail price of your book.
4. Ancillary services like editing, book cover design, and interior layout are competitively priced.
5. No minimum book purchase is required.

My advice when researching POD companies is to do a Google search and find out what others are saying about the company. The bottom line is: do your research, read the POD contract, and make sure that you are getting the best deal possible for yourself.

### *Virgin's Note*

*"Legally Blonde" was a self-published book by Amanda Brown. Her self-published book was made into the movie "Legally Blonde," starring Reese Witherspoon. After the movie was made, Plume published Brown's book, with an additional chapter on what's next for Elle Woods. Plume plans to publish the sequel called "Red, White & Blonde."*

### *Self Publisher's Checklist*

- ✓ *I have taken the Self Published Author's Quiz.*
- ✓ *I have researched the POD market using the Top Five Traits of a Great POD.*
- ✓ *I have chosen to proceed using a POD of my choice.*

# WHAT YOU WILL LEARN IN THIS CHAPTER

The author
platform

Understanding
what sells books

Determining my
reader and
conducting
market research

Growing my
author platform

# 3 FINDING YOUR MARKET

*"Gone are the days when self publishing was equal to self-defeating."*
~Paul Nathan, Columnist, *Publisher's Weekly*

## The Author Platform

What do Rush Limbaugh, Oprah Winfrey, Stephen King, Tom Clancy and Al Gore all have in common? They all have platforms, and big ones at that. If anyone tells you size doesn't matter, they weren't talking about an author's platform. Writers, actors or politicians with huge name recognition in the marketplace bring with them a *gi-mammoth* list of potential book buyers. That bevy of book buyers makes up the author's platform.

In years past, the mid-list author (an author selling less than 50,000 books), was the staple of the traditional publisher's inventory. However, over the past decade the publishing industry has become more competitive and publishing houses are looking for blockbuster books.

## Growing a Platform

Seth Godin, in his book *Tribes* talks about the importance of developing a group of people who look to you as a leader or the purveyor of information that they need.

Your platform is the group of people you're connected to or have influence over; it's your mailing list. They may be your friends on Facebook, names in your email list, or the member list of an organization that you belong to.

As a soon-to-be author, building your list (your platform) is job priority one! As an author you will need a Web site and social media skills. Here's the good news. As a self-published author, you don't have to compete with celebrity authors. All you have to do is sell your book, loads of them, to the people in your niche.

If your niche is 300,000 possible readers, and you sell your book to only 5 percent of that niche, you have sold 15,000 books! If you are making a $6 dollar profit on each book, you will have a gross profit of $90,000 dollars.

When you are building your platform, you are first and foremost a salesperson. One of the self-published authors in my writing group was able to garner 70 people to her local book reading. How did she do it? She told everyone she came into contact with that she was a published author; she gave them the name of her book, the Web site address (URL), the date, time and location of her next book reading. She advertised the event on her Facebook page and sent out emails to friends and relatives. The book store told her that the previous week they had had lower attendance for a book reading by a well-known author!

It's not who you are that will sell your books, but how hard you're willing to work and what you are willing to try. Your only limitation on how and where to sell your book is your own imagination.

### *Virgin's Note*

*One of the most effective and cheapest things I did to market this book was make one-hour presentations at libraries in my region. Although I didn't get paid for my mini self-publishing workshop, I did get the name of my book in the library newsletter that goes out to thousands of readers. At each mini-seminar, I passed around a sign-up sheet asking people for their names and email addresses, and if they would like to receive my newsletter. If I had a paid workshop scheduled, I announced that as well.*

## Who is Your Reader?

*Who is my reader?* It sounds like an easy question, but you need to be specific about the answer. Why? Your reader or your pool of potential readers must be large enough to sustain healthy book sales to make publishing and selling your book worthwhile. Your readers must be accessible using standard marketing techniques. If your book is about becoming a mountain climber's guide and your market is Himalayan Sherpas, then traditional marketing techniques won't work! The table below is a list of sites that can be useful in doing your market research.

| www.Fedstats.com | A conglomerate Web site with links to multiple government databases |
|---|---|
| www.Census.com | Useful for determining the demographics for a particular group (income levels, education, etc.) |
| www.infousa.com | Database of businesses in the U.S. Provides number of employees, gross sales and key personnel |
| ALA.org | Library Association Web site |
| *Gales Encyclopedia of Associations* | Lists all associations by subject in the U.S. |
| *International Book of Associations* | Lists all associations by subject internationally |
| *The Writer's Market* | A great database of magazines, including U.S. trade magazines |

**Figure 3.1**          *Table of references for market research*

## Finding Your Market

As a first-time author, you may not have a huge budget to place expensive ads in *Publisher's Weekly, Literary Journal* or other trade magazines; you will need to be more creative in finding your potential buyers. Here are some questions to ask yourself that will help you find your buyers:

- When writing my book, what reference materials, books, magazines, newspapers, blogs or periodicals did I read?
- What groups did I visit or join?
- What Web sites did I visit?
- In *Gales Encyclopedia of Associations*, which associations listed might be in my market?
- Where do my readers go to work, have fun, or just relax?

Make a comprehensive list of the Web sites, blogs, associations, and magazines that you believe your reader may read or belong to. For magazines, you can call and speak to the director of advertising. Tell them you are thinking about placing an ad in their publication. Ask them to send you a rate card and some sample back issues. Rate cards are often available on a publication's Web site. When you get the magazines, look at the sales ads and the classifieds in the back of the magazine. If you see the same ads over and over again, the advertising is working for them. A list from this magazine may be filled with people who want to buy your book.

You can buy a list from a local provider in your area. These tend to be cheaper than magazine lists, although they are not always as effective. I have purchased lists of 2,000 to 5,000 names for less than $300 from local list vendors.

 *Self Publisher's Checklist*

✓  *Chose a book topic.*
✓  *Narrow your focus.*
✓  *Research my reader.*
✓  *Prepare a list of associations to contact.*

# WHAT YOU WILL LEARN IN THIS CHAPTER

Front matter
and back matter

Book anatomy

Searchable title
and sub-title

BTIC

# 4   BOOK ANATOMY

*"The difference between the right word and the almost right word is the difference between lightning and a lightning bug."*

~Mark Twain

## Building Your Book

When I was researching this book, I read dozens of books, articles, research papers, blogs and Web sites on self publishing, marketing and other related topics. I interviewed self-published authors, POD printers, and researched technical references. It takes time to compile the data, organize it and put it into book form.

## BTIC

You don't have to work15 hours a day to write a book, but you had better work four to six hours every day over weeks and months. To complete any large writing project you should employ the BTIC principle: *butt time in chair.*

To keep track of my progress, I created an Excel spreadsheet that tracked my daily writing. Don't kid yourself; in order to write and finish a 200-plus page book you will need to make consistent progress each and every day. For me, the writing came in "shifts" during the day, rather than one huge block of time. There is no right or wrong here.

Stephen King, a prolific writer, says that a book can be written in a season—three to four months. Let me tell you from experience—if you write your book in a *season*, you will spend most of that season, sitting down!

I used a spreadsheet to track my progress. My goal was to write 500 words a day, six days a week. Logging each day's progress gave me real numbers, daily, of what I accomplished. The chart below is a portion of the spreadsheet I used to write this book. Here is what I tracked:

- Date
- Task – what I worked on that day or session
- Login and logout – When I started and finished
- Starting Wd Ct – Starting word count
- End Wd Ct – Ending word count for the session
- Week to Date, Month to Date and Project to Date were all running totals.

The sheet isn't magical, but it will give you something every writer needs—*accountability.* Remember the old Chinese proverb? You can eat an elephant—one bite at a time!

| DATE | Task | LOGIN | LOGOUT | Starting Wd Ct | End Wd Ct | session Wd Ct | Week to Date | Month to Date | Project to Date |
|---|---|---|---|---|---|---|---|---|---|
| January 28,2011 | writing copy | 11:14am | 11:15am | 38,713 | | 0 | 0 | 10,066 | 38,713 |
| January 28,2011 | isbn Websites, copyright site | 1:30pm | 2:05pm | 39159 | | 446 | 446 | 10,512 | 39,159 |
| January 28,2011 | writing | 4:00pm | 5:03pm | 40568 | | 1409 | 1,855 | 10,958 | 40,568 |
| January 28,2011 | writing last two chapters | 5:05pm | 5:26pm | 40,450 | | -118 | 1,737 | 12,813 | 40,450 |
| | general writing | | 12:00 AM | 41443 | | 993 | 2,730 | 14,550 | 41,443 |
| January 30,2011 | last two chapters | 1:05pm | | 41443 | 41965 | 522 | 3,252 | 17,280 | 41,443 |
| 3-Feb | last two chapters | 11:00am | 11:55am | 41965 | 41965 | 0 | 3,252 | 20,532 | 41,965 |
| 3-Feb-11 | Amazon chapter | 1:14pm | 3:39pm | 41965 | 43617 | 1652 | 4,904 | 23,784 | 41,965 |
| Feb 5 2011 | rewrites and editing | 4:29pm | 8:39pm | 43617 | 44293 | 676 | 5,580 | 28,688 | 43,617 |
| | rewrite chapt on CS finish marketing | 9:00pm | 10:47pm | 44293 | 44885 | 592 | 6,172 | 34,268 | 44,293 |
| Feb 5 2011 | last chapter writing | 11:00pm | 11:35pm | 44685 | 45768 | 883 | 7,055 | 40,440 | 44,885 |
| Feb 5 2011 | amazon chapter/social media | 1:00 AM | 2:47am | 45768 | 56735 | 10967 | 18,022 | 47,495 | 45,768 |
| Feb 8 2011 | final chapters | 6pm | 12am | 45768 | 49635 | 3867 | 21,889 | 65,517 | 45,768 |
| 9-Feb-11 | final chapter/ end first draft | 2:36pm | | 49635 | | | 21,889 | 87,406 | 49,635 |

Note: Final word count of first draft was 49,635

Final word count second draft was 46,224 m- about a 7% reduction in word count

# Book Anatomy

Books have supplemental pages. Not all books have all the supplemental pages. The pages you include can vary depending on the market you are trying to reach.

## Marketing Pages

As a self-published writer, you are a business person. The marketing pages of your book help you sell more books. As a self-published author, you can pick and choose which pages you want to include. The pages listed below, "contact the author" and "warning and disclaimers," should be included in your book.

### Bulk Purchase Instructions

Some customers may want to buy multiple copies (bulk) of your book at a significant discount. Let them know that discounted bulk purchases are available and make it easy for them to contact you.

### Contact the Author

Consider adding a "contact the author" page. (This can be on the same page as the bulk purchase notice.) As an unabashed, self-promoting, self-published author, you should always make it easy for your readers to contact you. Include your Web site and an email address.

To keep readers coming to your Web site, post updates to the information contained in your book and keep a current speaking schedule on your site. Make yourself accessible to your readers and they will love you for it!

### Warning and Disclaimer

If you are writing a technical book, you should include this page. Talk to your attorney and give some thought to a disclaimer page. For help, go to Amazon.com or the book store and read the warning and disclaimer pages of other books.

## Front Matter

What is front matter? Any page that appears before the text in chapter one of your book is a part of the front matter. It may include a copyright page, foreword and one or two introduction pages. If you are writing non-fiction, the front matter can be quite lengthy. Your book, depending on the genre, may use some or all of these pages.

### Copyright Page

All books have a copyright page. The copyright page has the ISBN (Industry Standard Book Number), LCCN (Library of Congress Number), the edition, publisher's name and other listing information. We will talk about the ISBNs and LCCNs in later chapters.

### *Virgin's Note*

*All parts of the front matter, excluding the copyright page and interior cover page should be referenced in the contents. Page numbering for the contents and front matter can be formatted differently from the rest of your book. Remember, the more professional your book appears, the more potential buyers will want to purchase your book.*

## Blurbs

A blurb is a quotation or series of quotations or testimonials from people who have read and enjoyed your book. Testimonials sell books. The more blurbs you have, the better. Use three to five of your best blurbs on the back cover of your book. On the first odd-numbered page of your book after your title page, list all of the blurbs you collected, starting with the most recognized people first.

Seek blurbs from people who are authority figures, experts or celebrities in the field. The more name recognition they will have with your potential readers, the better.

 ***Virgin's Note***

*When making your list of people who may provide blurbs, write down 25 to 30 names and contact them all in hopes of getting five to eight responses. Let them know that you will send their complimentary copy of your book as soon as it is published—then make sure that you do it!*

## Interior Cover Page

The interior cover page is a black and white copy of the front cover of your book and should appear on the first odd-numbered page, just inside your book cover.

## Table of Contents

All books should have a table of contents (TOC). The TOC is the backbone of your book. If your book is non-fiction, a comprehensive TOC works best. The more content you can provide in the table of contents, the easier it is for your reader to determine if the information they are looking for is in your book!

### *Virgin's Note*

*The TOC is the second place the potential buyer examines when making a purchase. Online shoppers are more prone to search the TOC to verify that the specific information they need is covered in your book. If the buyer doesn't see it in the TOC, he or she will assume it is not in your book! Make your TOCs comprehensive.*

## Foreword

The foreword is generally written by someone else, not the author. It details how the book came to be written. The person writing the foreword gives information about his or her connection with the author, which gives the book credibility and authority.

## Preface

A preface is written by the author and is usually signed and dated. The preface should come before the introduction and should tell the reader about how the book came into being.

### Introduction

This is usually written by the author and is more detailed than the preface. It introduces the reader to the content of your book.

## Timing

When it comes to soliciting components of your front matter like the foreword, blurbs, or testimonials, timing is important. As soon as you have a galley copy of your book ready, share it with the people who will be writing the blurbs, foreword or testimonials. Give them some guidelines on the length that you want and a delivery date. Solicit these folks two or three months before your publication date.

## Handling Graphics

Artwork should be crisp and clean. If your book is in black and white, use grayscale graphics. Word can convert a color graphic to grayscale. Graphics in your book should be 300 ppi which means 300 pixels per inch to avoid blurry graphics.

## Back Matter

Back matter consists of the pages at the back of the book, after the end of the text, including the back cover.

## Epilogue

An epilogue is used for books of fiction and is written to bring closure to the story.

## Afterword

Also used for fiction books, an afterword concludes the story after a long period of time has elapsed.

## Appendix

The appendix is supplemental information included in the book to enhance the book's usefulness. Appendices can be pages of Web sites, government resources, agencies, associations, groups or other resources useful to your reader.

## Glossary

The glossary is a set of definitions of words used in the book.

## Bibliography

The bibliography cites other sources. If you have cited portions of other authors' works in your book, list their names and their works in the bibliography. To see the format for bibliography listings, visit:

**en.wikipedia.org/wiki/Bibliography**

## Index

An index is a listing of key words that appear in the body of your text. Many POD printers offer an indexing service. If you are using

Microsoft Word, there is built-in index function that works well. Hiring a professional indexer can be costly.

### About the Author

You should include this page in the back of your book. Add a picture that is professional, but not staged. The author page is not a resume but an "artist's statement" that tells the reader how you came to write the book.

*Virgin's Note*

*If you are publishing a non-fiction, how-to or reference book, and want to access the library market, include an appendix, bibliography and an index. Librarians want resource books for their patrons. One way to make your non-fiction book stand out as a resource is to include an index and additional resource pages.*

## Choosing a Title

Give your book a title as soon as you can. This is your "working title." When the book is finished, the working title may change. If you are writing fiction, don't choose a title that gives away the ending.

*Virgin's Note*

*As an author, your name and the name of your book are an intricate part of your overall marketing plan. As soon as you have chosen a permanent title for your book, it should be registered immediately with a domain name service like GoDaddy or Bluehost. You should also register your name as a domain. If you write under James Smith and your book is called How to be a Top Salesman, then you should have two domain names or URLs: www.jamesmith.com and www.howtobeatopsalesman.com and possibly www.topsalesman.com*

## The Searchable Sub-title

The sub-title is important. While the title points to the book's subject, the sub-title tells the story. Amazon searches both titles and sub-titles.

When you enter a search word for a book on Amazon, it searches first for the title, then the sub-title. Let's say that you have written a book about poodle dogs called, *Training Your Poodle.* Your sub-title is, "*How to breed, board and sell poodle dogs.*" If I am searching on Amazon for a book about boarding poodles, and I type in "boarding poodles," your book will come up since the words "board" and "poodle" are in your sub-title.

To take full advantage of Amazon's search algorithm, write a sub-title that uses several key search words for your book. This will increase the odds of Amazon listing your book as a search match.

### Self Publisher's Checklist

- ✓ Choose a working title for your book.
- ✓ Develop your sub-title, keeping in mind search algorithms on Amazon.
- ✓ Create a Word.doc file called CreateSpace setup.doc.
- ✓ Save your title on one line and your sub-title on the next line in the createspacesetup.doc.
- ✓ Get a high quality photograph (300 ppi) or snapshot of you that is well done without being stiff or staged.
- ✓ Prepare your "About the Author" page and save it to CreateSpacesetup.doc under your title and sub-title.
- ✓ If you have been working on your book, it should be in one Word document file. ( Do not use multiple files when working with Word to lay out your book.)
- ✓ Have a list of 25 to 30 names of people who may provide blurbs. Be ready to mail review copies to this list once the manuscript is edited.

"Writing is one of the few professions in which you can psychoanalyze yourself, get rid of hostilities and frustrations in public, and get paid for it."

~Octavia Butler

# WHAT YOU WILL LEARN FROM THIS CHAPTER

First draft and
second draft

Editing

Hiring an editor

What editors do

# 5 EDITING

## The First Draft

Now it's time to talk about the most important aspect of crafting your book—*editing*. If your book is written, then you have completed your first draft. As you write your book for the first time, you are writing in a near "stream-of-consciousness" mode. That is the way a first draft should be written. I have seen so many writers try to finish a first draft without success because they try to do two things at once, write and edit.

Ernest Hemingway, a master of writing, and of first drafts, was once credited as saying, "All first drafts are shit." The key to completing your book is completing your first draft. Don't try to edit before the first draft is complete. This can be hard to resist, but resist you must!

If you are writing your first draft and you find you are missing some data or you have to research a point—don't stop writing. Simply insert a note to yourself in the text by typing in all caps, "Research later" or "Insert info here." Mark the note in red so that when you are ready for the second draft, you can do the research.

Once your first draft is finished, put the manuscript aside for a period of time. Depending on your publication schedule, that may be two to six weeks or longer. This will give you a more objective look at your work when you are ready to re-read the book and prepare the second draft.

## The Second Draft

When you have completed your first draft, set your book aside. If you have the time in your publication schedule, leave your manuscript in a drawer for at least two weeks. Don't look at it at all.

When you are ready, take it out of the drawer, sit down, and read the book through, in one sitting. This will fix in your mind a clearer perspective of how the book flows. Keep a legal pad beside you and make notes (be sure to list page numbers) of things that strike you as incongruent, or need to be checked, or that require additional research.

## Five Steps to a Second Draft

1. Correct all misspellings, typos, and punctuation errors.
2. Make extensive notes on anything that strikes you as inconsistent, unclear, or wrong—be sure to include page numbers.
3. Keep a positive mindset; don't beat yourself up over your mistakes. The second draft was made for correcting mistakes.
4. Relentlessly remove passages, sentences or phrases that don't move the book forward. Always ask, "Does my reader need to know this?" If the answer is no, then take it out!

5. Your second draft should be at least 10 percent smaller than your first draft. Stephen King says in his book *On Writing,* "...the second draft equals the first draft minus 20 percent."

## Reference Books

William Strunk Jr. was an English professor at Cornell University. In 1919, he wrote a book on style which he used in his English class. It has become a classic reference book for any serious writer. Now, in its third edition, *The Elements of Style* gives us some sterling advice.

## Strunk's Four Rules

1. Don't overwrite or overstate.
2. Avoid the use of qualifiers like *rather, very, little, pretty.*
3. Write with nouns and verbs.
4. Don't over construct or explain too much and use direct, simple language.

Use these rules and the five steps above to create a tighter, more streamlined second draft.

Here are some books that you should have on your shelf as you navigate your second draft:

1. *On Writing* by Stephen King
2. *The Elements of Style* by William Strunk and E.B. White
3. *The New York Times Manual of Style and Usage*
4. *The Chicago Manual of Style*

## Favorite Readers

Your second draft is finished. You are ready to get input from favorite readers. Choose your favorite readers carefully. Your Aunt Nelly who loves everything you do is not a good candidate. I like what one writer said; I paraphrase, "Find the meanest SOB you can find and let him be your reader." Favorite readers should be objective and able to give you feedback—good or bad. If favorite readers consistently have trouble with one chapter, phrase or section of your book, fix it. If they think it could be better organized, listen. Why? Because they are reading your book with objectivity—something you, as the creator of the book, no longer have. Your favorite readers should know ahead of time that you need your book read right away. Give them a target date, and if you don't get all of your manuscripts back on time, move on. If you get negative feedback, don't be offended. It will help you create a better, more organized, more readable book which will translate to more book sales.

Too many writers think their book is their baby—it's not—your book is your business.

## Auto Crit

If you would like to try some automated software to help you edit, try **www.autocrit.com**. You can try a free trial of 400 words and up to three submissions per day for a total of three reports only. If you like it, then you can sign up for one of their paid plans.

## Reading Out Loud

I know it sounds weird, but reading your book out loud to someone whose opinion you trust will help you improve the quality of your book. Why? A friend of mine who is a counselor and medical expert tells me that reading out loud engages a different part of your brain and can give you more of what all writers long for: *objectivity.* If you get tired of reading yourself, then ask your listener to read the chapters to you. This can also help you hear the flow of your book. If your reader stumbles over a certain passage, it may be because the flow is not there.

### *Virgin's Note*

*I know one author who gave her book to ten favorite readers. She received all of them back within two months except one. One year later the person called her and said, "I have your manuscript back, all marked and ready to go!" The author, whose book had already been through the editing process months before and was now published, simply smiled, accepted the manuscript and said, "Thank you." Not all favorite readers will get your book read in a timely fashion. If they don't, move on!*

## Hiring an Editor

Now that you have feedback from your favorite readers and have made the required adjustments, it's time to hire a professional editor. You cannot edit your own work. You are too close to the work, and you have looked at the errors so long that your mind will literally see the error as it should be written.

Editing rule of thumb:  *If you are not a professional editor, don't edit your own work. If you are a professional editor, don't edit your own work.*

## What Editors Do

What can you expect from a professional editor? I will tell you what my editor Susan Lindsey told me. First and foremost, they will check your manuscript for the five Cs — *clarity, chronology, coherency, consistency* and *correctness.*

An editor will fix spelling, grammar, and punctuation mistakes and edit for point of view, verb tense, and inconsistencies; check the logical flow of information or plot; and alert you to inconsistencies and awkward transitions.

Charges for editing can vary. If you are using a POD printer to self publish your book, your POD will provide fee-based editing services. These can run from $400 plus for a book under 200 pages to thousands of dollars for a larger book. Remember, your editor is your partner in creating the best book possible. An editor's advice can be invaluable and make the difference between an OK book, and a great book.

If you are thinking of hiring an independent editor, the fees vary, depending on the complexity of the text, the skill of the writer, word count and other factors. *Writer's Market* magazine publishes an updated list of fees for services annually.

When hiring an editor, always ask for a written proposal and make sure you understand what services you will receive.

### *Self Publisher's Checklist*

- ✓ *Have a professionally edited manuscript in a Word.doc file.*
- ✓ *Have several galley copies prepared to be sent to blurb candidates.*
- ✓ *Prepare a draft letter or email to send to prospective reviewers.*

# WHAT YOU WILL LEARN FROM THIS CHAPTER

Using Word

The tools you need to self publish

Using a PDF conversion software

Organizing with Excel

# 6  TOOLS FOR PUBLISHING

*" A lot of people ask me if I were shipwrecked, and could only have one book, what would it be? I always say <u>How to Build a Boat</u>."*

~Stephen Wright

## Layout Tools

By this chapter, you should be in the final stages of writing your book. Before you set up your book on CreateSpace, there are some things you must do to make the set-up process go more smoothly.

If we were building a bookcase, we would first assemble our tools. Self publishing is no different. As a reminder, the software I have chosen is not the most expensive or the cheapest. It was chosen based on my criteria of "best functionality for the least money."

## Word

Creating an interior layout (the inside of the book) using any software can be daunting. When I created my first interior layout in Word, it wasn't easy. The good news is, if you stick with it, you can create a professional layout with Word. The instructions in this book are for a basic layout.

The instructions here are written for Word 2007. If you are using Word 2003, the instructions will be about the same (some menu names may be different). Microsoft 2010 will work also, but again, some commands may be different.

For those of you with fatter wallets, Adobe In Design or Quark Express are great programs for doing an interior layout. I chose Word because it is less expensive than the alternatives, and most people already have it installed on their computers.

If you have the budget and are technically savvy, Adobe In Design CS5™ is a comprehensive desktop publisher. It costs $369. If you are writing a technical book, with drawings and lots of graphics, In Design™ is a better way to go.

### *Virgin's Note*

> *If you prefer not to do the interior layout yourself, you can opt to have CreateSpace do the interior layout for you. The charge for interior layout starts at $299 and goes up, depending on the complexity of the layout.*

## Bluebeam PDF Revu™

When you self publish a book, you need to create a PDF file (more on that in Chapter 12). Keeping in mind my criteria of *best functionality for lowest price,* I like Bluebeam PDF Revu™, Standard Edition. A licensed copy retails for $99. It's easy to use and creates a clean PDF file. You can purchase a licensed copy online at **www.bluebeam.com** or try their 30- day free trial.

When I created my first book layout for Women Who Write, I was terrified. There was no budget for buying Adobe Acrobat™, so I Googled *"cheap or free PDF software."* That's how I found Bluebeam. Bluebeam also makes a free PDF program called PrimoPDF (www.primoPDF.com). PrimoPDF works fine for converting Word documents to PDF for everyday use, but *don't use free software to create your pre-publication file.* The PDF file for a print-on-demand printer must be top quality.

## Organizing with Excel

When I wrote this book I started a spreadsheet. I used the spreadsheet to keep track of books cited in my manuscript, useful Web sites, and reference books for authors. When the book was finished, these spreadsheets made it easy to create my appendices and the bibliography.

If you are using Word, you can use the *citation* command to keep track of your bibliography. The command is cumbersome and hard to use at first. If you persevere, it gets easier.

### *Virgin's Note*

*Now that you are writing your book, it's time to back up your files. Recently I brought my laptop into the classroom at a local university where I was presenting a seminar on self publishing. As soon as I turned on the computer, I got the dreaded blue screen. I was never able to access my laptop or my PowerPoint presentation. Thankfully I had printed copies of the PP presentation, so I gave each attendee a copy. Later, I discovered that my hard drive had failed. I was able to retrieve my data intact, but if I hadn't made frequent backups, I could have been in serious trouble. Your book is an investment of* *weeks, months or years.  Protect that investment by multiple backups. Email your manuscript to yourself periodically. Use flash drives and CD's. If you can afford an off-site backup system like Carbonite—do it ($55 annually for one PC). Another alternative is to purchase an external hard drive for your laptop or computer (under $100).*

### *Self Publisher's Checklist*

✓  *Obtain a licensed copy of Bluebeam Revue PDF.*
✓  *Prepare a list of recommended reading (this will be used later for your appendices).*
✓  *Compile a list of cited books complete with ISBN number, edition, title, author/s and publisher.*
✓  *Create a spreadsheet list of associations, groups, Web sites or organizations that you want to recommend to your readers.*

*"What we think, or what we know, or what we believe is, in the end, of little consequence. The only consequence is what we do."*

~John Ruskin

# WHAT YOU WILL LEARN IN THIS CHAPTER

Copyright and the
Fair Use doctrine

How to register a
copyright with
copyright.gov

Author's rights

CCC (Copyright
Clearance Center)
and protecting
international
rights

# 7 COPYRIGHT AND FAIR USE

*"But here's the thing: what you do as a screenwriter is you sell your copyright. As a novelist, as a poet, as a playwright, you maintain your copyright."*
~Beth Henley

## Copyright 101

Here are the quick answers for the type A personalities among my readers:

Should you copyright your work?
Yes.
Does it cost a lot of money?
No.
Can it be done online?
Yes.
What is the cost?
$35
Where do I go?
**www.copyright.gov**

Those are the quick answers. More detail-oriented writers should read the rest of the chapter.

## What is Copyright?

Copyright is a form of protection provided by the laws of the United States to the authors of "original works of authorship." This includes literary works, dramatic, musical, artistic, and certain other intellectual works. Copyright protection covers both published and unpublished works. The Copyright Act of 1976 gives the owner of the copyright the exclusive right to authorize others to do the following:

- Reproduce the work
- Prepare derivative works
- Distribute copies to the public by sale or other means of transfer
- Perform or display the work publicly

These rights are limited. One major limitation is the doctrine of "fair use," which we will discuss later in this chapter.

You may have heard people say, "I don't need to copyright my book because it's protected when it's created. If I want to protect it, I can put it an envelope and mail it to myself." It is true that a work is copyrighted when it is created. Publication of your work is not required for that work to be copyrighted. There are, however, distinct advantages to registering your copyrighted work with the government copyright office. If we think of copyright as a bundle of rights that protects the work from infringement, then registration of the copyright strengthens those rights.

## What's Not Protected?

Not everything is protected by copyright. There are several categories of material that fall into the unprotected range.

- Works that have not been fixed in a tangible form

- Titles, names, short phrases and slogans
- Ideas, procedures, methods, systems, processes and concepts
- Works that consist entirely of information that is commonly available such as standard calendars, height and weight charts, lists or tables taken from public documents or other common sources

## How to Copyright

The copyright office of the United States can be accessed online at **www.copyright.gov.** While you can register your work by mail, it is cheaper and simpler to register the work online. The form is several pages long, but many of the questions are repetitive and not all of them will apply to every work. You can print their frequently asked question from the Web site.

The folks at the copyright office are easy to work with and you can call to get help with completing the form. The number is busy, so call early. Their phone number is (202) 707-3000.

## Notice of Copyright

The use of a copyright notice is no longer required under U.S. law. It can still be beneficial to use it. Because notice was once required by law, its use is still relevant to the copyright status of older works.[1]

Use of notice may be important because it lets the public know that a work is copyrighted, identifies the owner of the copyright, and shows the year of first publication. It is important to note that if a work is infringed and proper notice was given via a copyright notice, then the infringer cannot claim in court that they did not know the work was copyrighted.

---

[1] See 1976 Copyright Act

The format of copyright notice matters. Here is the correct format.

The notice for visual perceptible copies should contain all three of the following elements:

1. The symbol © (the letter "c" in a circle), or the word "Copyright," or the abbreviation "Copr"
2. The year of the first publication of the work
3. The name of the owner of the copyright. (Example: © 2010 *Your Name Here)*

### *Virgin's Note*

*Here is a cautionary tale of why authors should take copyright notice seriously. A writer had been working on a collection of stories based on his observances of a neighbor who lived next door. As he worked on these stories and they grew into a collection, he considered publishing them. The writer had joined a critique group and began to share the stories with the group. One of the members in the critique group, having listened to several readings, published a book using the same idea down to the title. Might this writer have been more able to defend his work had he included a copyright notice? I think so!*

## Permissions

In the process of writing your book, you may use another person's material to clarify a point or to illustrate an idea. When you do this, give proper attribution. This simply means that if you quote the work of another, you must say that the work is from that person. Any quotation taken directly from someone else's work should be given credit, in writing, citing their work and where it appeared. Even when you have given proper attribution, you are limited on how much you can quote someone else in your work without their express written permission.

When quoting another's work, keep it brief and only use the minimum that you need to make your point. If you overstep and use too much, even with attribution, you can put yourself in legal jeopardy. The cardinal rule is to always give credit and don't use too much.

## Fair Use and Plagiarism

When you steal someone else's words, work or materials without giving proper attribution, then you are presenting the work as your own. This is plagiarism. In the publishing world this is a major offense and should be avoided at all costs. Plagiarism is illegal and it can be devastating to a writer's career.

The best way to stay out of trouble is to carefully document your source. Here are some examples of when you need to document:

- ✓ Quoting from a book, newspaper or magazine article
- ✓ Quoting from a TV show, blog, Web page or advertisement
- ✓ Quoting words spoken during an interview, done either by you or by someone else
- ✓ Quoting someone speaking at a press conference or giving a speech
- ✓ Reproducing art work or a graphical image

Ideas cannot be copyrighted, but specific text can be. Facts are not protected and can be used by used by anyone. To learn more about plagiarism and copyright issues, visit these Web sites:

**www.copyright.gov**

**www.plagiarism.org/faq.html**

## Registering Copyright

Even though the law doesn't require copyright registration, copyright law provides several advantages to works that are registered.

- Registration creates a public record of the copyright claim.
- Copyright registration is required before an infringement suit can be filed.
- If made before or within five years of the creation of the work, registration establishes *prima facie* evidence in court of the validity of the copyright.
- If the registration is made within three months after publication of the work or prior to an infringement, statutory damages and attorney's fees will be available to the copyright owner.
- Registration allows the owner of the copyright to record the registration with the U.S. Customs Service for protection against the importation of infringing copies.

## How the Process Works

The registration application includes three elements: a completed application form, a non-refundable filing fee, and a non-returnable deposit—which is a copy of the work being registered or "deposited" with the Copyright Office.

With an online or paper application, you can expect to receive:

- A letter, call or email from a Copyright Office staff member if further information is needed.

- A Certificate of Registration indicating the work has been registered, or a letter explaining why the application has been rejected.

Online registration is the preferred way to register basic claims for literary works. It requires a lower filing fee and has faster processing times.

For literary works, send hard copy deposits to:

Library of Congress
U.S. Copyright Office
101 Independence Avenue SE
Washington, DC 20559-6222
www.Copyright.gov
(202) 707-3000

The current registration fee for online registration is $35. When I spoke with a Copyright Office staff member while doing research for this book, I was told that the process can take as long as four to nine months from the time the office receives the application until you receive your registration. I was also told that the work does not have to be complete, but should be substantially complete, to apply for registration. I spoke with two different staff members and was given different information. One staff person stated that 50 to 70 percent complete is all that is required, and another said that the first sentence would be enough. If you intend to send an incomplete work, keep in mind that in the case of a conflict, the most "finished" work will receive the copyright registration. For example, a perfect bound deposit is considered more complete than a galley.

Registered copyrights last for your lifetime plus 70 years. According to the Copyright Office official flyer, *Copyright Basics*, copyrights may be bequeathed by will or passed as personal property by the applicable laws of intestate succession.

## Copyright Clearance Center

The Copyright Clearance Center is not connected with the U.S. Copyright Office. It is a separate entity with offices around the world. As we have discussed, in the United States you can't copy someone else's work, at least not substantial portions of it without permission from the copyright holder. In other countries, this practice is legal provided the person copying the material pays a fee.

In other countries, these fees are collected on behalf of the copyright holder and disbursed through an central agency called the Reproductive Rights Organization (RRO). The fees are collected by the RRO and then the royalties are paid to the copyright holders in that country. If the copyrighted work is foreign, the fees are sent to the RRO in the country of use, to be distributed there. This is great news for Americans, because it means that U.S. writers can collect fees charged in foreign countries for reproducing their work.

We aren't talking just book excerpts here, but anything that you have written that might be photocopied and distributed in a foreign country. This includes material from blogs, e-books or Web sites.

You need to make sure that your work published online can be clearly attributed to you, and that you have supplied an address where the royalties can be sent. The best way to ensure payment is to sign up with the RRO agency in the U.S. which is called the Copyright Clearance Center (CCC). To learn more, visit **www.copyright.com**.

When completing the form, use your personal name and your publishing name or publishing company name as the organization. Even though you have never signed up you may already have an account. Check for an existing account. There's nothing wrong with having more than one account. You could have one under your publishing name and one under your publishing company's name. You can set up direct deposit if you are comfortable giving them your banking information or you can have checks mailed to you.

Listed below are several Web sites to get the registration process started. It may take a little time, but it will be worth it in the long run, especially if you plan to publish your works internationally. The primary site to investigate other agencies is the International Federation of Reproduction Rights Organizations or IFRRO. Their Web site is **www.ifrro.org.**

**Web sites***:*

Australia                    Copyright Agency Limited (CAL)
                             **www.copyright.com.au/**

Canada                       Access Copyright
                             **www.accesscopyright.ca/**

New Zealand:                 Copyright Licensing LTD. (CLL)
                             **www.copyright.co.nz/**

Keep your address information current and correct. If you publish in the United Kingdom, you can enroll in the Author's Licensing and Collecting Society (ACLS) and the Publishers Licensing Society or PLS.

### *Virgin's Note*

*To become more familiar with copy reproduction rights and copyright issues at stake for writers today, download Google's Book Settlement. If you wish to, CreateSpace will apply for a copyright registration for your book on your behalf. The cost is $75.*

 *Self Publisher's Checklist*

✓ *Download a Copyright application from www.copyright.gov.*
✓ *Complete the Copyright application form.*
✓ *Register with Copyright Clearance Center/s, if applicable.*
  *Note: if you have made the decision to let CreateSpace register*
  *a copyright on your behalf, that step will be done when you set*
  *up your author's account in CreateSpace (See Part Two.)*

*"If there's a book you really want to read, but it hasn't been written yet, then you must write it."*

~Toni Morrison

# WHAT YOU WILL LEARN FROM THIS CHAPTER

ISBN, LCCN and
Publisher of
Record

Taking care of the
numbers

PCN and
application for
publication

World Cat

# 8 GETTING THE NUMBERS

*"I'm writing a book. I've got the page numbers done."* ~Stephen Wright

This chapter, *Getting the Numbers*, is one of the hardest chapters to master if you are a first-time, self-publishing author. For that reasonn I am splitting the chapter into two sections. Section One is for first-time authors who plan to write only one book. Section Two is for career authors who plan on publishing more than one book, in more than one media, or who want to establish their own publishing company.

## Section One

Your manuscript is complete and professionally edited, and now it is time to get the numbers. What do you do? If you are going to publish only one book, then I recommend that you let CreateSpace provide both your ISBN and apply for your LCCN. The ISBN is free from CreateSpace and the cost for applying to the Library of Congress for a pre-assigned LCCN is $75. This makes the cost of publishing your book $114. Here's how that number breaks down:

| | |
|---|---|
| One-time fee for CreateSpace Pro Plan | $39 |
| ISBN | Free[2] |
| LCCN application | $75 |
| **Total Cost** | **$114** |

(The CreateSpace Pro Plan gives you the best pricing on author copies. It is a one-time fee and is well worth the money.)

Your only remaining costs will be for services that you decide to purchase instead of doing them yourself. Here is a list of services you may want.

## Interior Layout

CreateSpace interior book layouts start at $299 for a basic layout. A custom interior layout starts at $499.

## Kirkus Review

A Kirkus Review is a paid review that costs $250. There is no guarantee that the review will be a good one. Many in the industry think that a paid review isn't necessary.

## Book Cover Design

Basic book covers start at $499 and up.

---

[2] Before you decide to take advantage of a free ISBN number from a POD printer, be sure you understand the facts. See "Publisher of Record" later in this chapter.

***Virgin's Note***
*Because you can publish your book so cheaply with CreateSpace, it is an excellent way for small non-profits and 501(c)(3)s to publish a book and sell it as a fundraiser.*

## Section Two

This section is for those of you who are professional writers and intend to publish several books in your lifetime. If that is your goal, then you should consider forming your own publishing company. This section briefly discusses how to form an LLC or a corporation for your publishing business, but for more details and advice on which corporate structure works best for you, consult an accountant or attorney.

## When to Get What

There are two numbers that your book should have, an ISBN (Industry Standard Book Number), and an LCCN[3] (Library of Congress Control Number). To sell your book in bookstores, specialty stores, or online it must have an ISBN. CreateSpace can furnish one or both numbers for you, at your option. If you plan to sell your book to libraries, an LCCN is important.

---

[3] LCCN can also be referred to as LCN for Library Control Number. They are the same number.

## ISBN

The ISBN is a 13-digit number that uniquely identifies your book internationally. R.R. Bowker, LLC (www.Bowker.com) is the agency that sells ISBNs to publishers and individual authors in the U.S. market.

All books sold in America, whether in a bookstore, a retail store or online, must have an ISBN before the book is published. Go to Bowker's Web site at **www.bowker.com** to obtain your ISBN.

Many print-on-demand vendors, including CreateSpace, will provide an ISBN number free of charge. You should read the entire chapter before deciding to allow your POD to provide an ISBN number. Most POD printers will also apply for a Library of Congress number on your behalf.

## What do the Numbers Mean?

There are four parts to an ISBN:

1. Group or country identifier
2. Publisher identifier
3. The number that identifies a particular title or edition of a title
4. A single digit at the end of the ISBN which validates the ISBN (the check digit)

If you have decided to start your own publishing company, you will have to pay for your ISBN. Individuals pay $125 for each number while publishers can purchase a block of ISBNs at discounted prices.[4]

---

[4] Publishers can purchase a block of 10 ISBNs for $250. See "Publisher of Record."

## Publisher of Record

Your book, throughout its print life, will be identified by its ISBN. ISBNs are assigned to each media version of your book. For example, if your book is available as a print book, e-book and an audio book, you will have three different ISBNs. Second editions of the same book use a different ISBN. (Print-on-demand technology is beginning to change this industry practice.) Using unique ISBNs for each media type and edition ensures accurate tracking and sales data.

Bowker sells ISBNs to individuals and to publishers. Individual authors can purchase an ISBN for $125. Publishers can purchase ISBNs in bulk, 10, 100 or 1000 at a time. A bulk purchase of ten numbers is $250; 100 numbers cost $500; and 1,000 numbers cost a dollar each.

The owner of the ISBN (you as the author, a publishing company, or the POD vendor) is called the *publisher of record.*

Why is this important? The publisher of record will be listed in *Books In Print* and all other databases as the publisher. As a self-published author you may want your name or the name of your publishing company as the publisher of record. CreateSpace's contract also specifies that if you use their ISBN (which they provide for free*),* your book cannot be transferred to another printer.

## ISBN Registration

ISBN numbers are purchased online through Bowker. You must first set up an account at **http://myidentifiers.com** (a landing page on Bowker.com). Once the account is set up you can purchase your ISBNs online from this site. The ISBNs appear in your account almost instantly, but it can take up to 24 hours to receive them.

Note: If you are letting CreateSpace supply your ISBN (free of charge), then your ISBN will be assigned automatically during the setup process.

## Assigning an ISBN

The process of linking the publication data of your book with the ISBN number is called assigning. Don't attempt to assign an ISBN before your book is published. The ISBN, combined with the barcode, is shown in the lower left or right corner of the back cover of your book. CreateSpace will provide a barcode so don't purchase one from Bowker.

Once your book is ready to be published, you will submit the book information to Bowker. Registering or assigning this information links your book and its information to a particular ISBN. It allows Bowker to enter your book's information into *Books In Print*. Listing your book in *Books In Print* makes it more discoverable by bookstores and libraries.

## Completing Title Registration

Go to **www.myidentifiers.com**, enter your user name and password, and log in under *My Account*. To access the Book Title Form, click on the blank subject line next to the ISBN you wish to register. This will bring up the next page which is the online form.

The book title form is two pages long. Be sure to scroll down below the SAVE button to enter pricing information. When entering the price of your book, don't use the dollar sign.

When asked about markets add only those markets in which you will sell.

If you have successfully completed the form, you should see a yellow circle with a black triangle to the left of your title name. This means that your title is processing and this will change to a green circle the following business day. A red circle means there is an error.

## Books In Print

Books In Print is an online database maintained by Bowker. The Books In Print database is accessed by publishers, librarians and booksellers all over the country. By completing the book information form, you enter your book's bibliographical data into the Books In Print database. The chart below shows the flow of information through the bowker.com site.

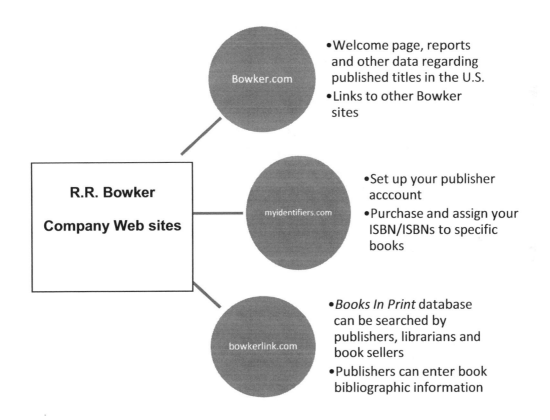

Bowker.com
- Welcome page, reports and other data regarding published titles in the U.S.
- Links to other Bowker sites

R.R. Bowker

Company Web sites

myidentifiers.com
- Set up your publisher acccount
- Purchase and assign your ISBN/ISBNs to specific books

bowkerlink.com
- *Books In Print* database can be searched by publishers, librarians and book sellers
- Publishers can enter book bibliographic information

## Me—a Publisher?

Should you go to the trouble and expense of starting your own publishing company? Only you can answer that question. I recommend that you speak with your accountant or tax attorney to get the best advice. Starting your own publishing company is not for the one-time, self-published author. If you are a career writer and plan to write more books, then starting your own publishing company makes sense.

## Starting a Publishing Company

You can register most business entities with the Secretary of State Web site in your state. Go to the Secretary of State's site and look for business licenses. Most state Web sites will let you print the form you need to start your business. You can then complete the form and mail it to the Secretary of State with your check.

You will also need to apply for an EIN (employer identification number). This can be done online also and is a separate transaction from setting up the publishing company. A Federal Tax ID number is also known as an Employer Identification Number (EIN). It is a nine-digit number valid in all states for banking, tax filing and other business purposes.

Here is the Web site for the EIN:

**www.irs.gov/businesses/small/article/0,,id=102767,00.html**

If your name is Dan Wilson, don't name your publishing company Wilson Publishing. That will make it obvious to people that your book is self-published. Naming your company after your surname makes your company harder to sell down the road. Choose a name that is unrelated to your name. The cost to establish a company can vary. There are also annual fees involved in maintaining your business identity entity, so check with your accountant or tax attorney before you make a decision.

### *Virgin's Note*

*Remember that if a traditional publisher or a movie producer or someone else wants to purchase rights to your book to do a movie, or some other type of purchase, they will contact the publisher of record, not the author. Having CreateSpace as the publisher of record will also tell the Library of Congress that your book is self-published and reduce your chances of being included in the LOC catalog.*

## Barcodes

You can obtain a barcode directly from Bowker or from your POD printer. Bowker will charge a small one-time fee for a barcode ($25), but most PODs will supply the barcode for free.

A barcode is essentially a price tag. CreateSpace will provide the barcode once you have entered your book's ISBN and list price online during the CreateSpace set up. For more information on barcodes, see **www.myidentifiers.com** and click on the Barcodes tab.

## Library of Congress Number (LCCN)

If you want to market your book to libraries, you must have a Library of Congress Control number. You must apply for an LCCN *before* your book is published. Don't get confused if you see the LCCN called the LCN. They are the same.

*A Library of Congress Catalog Control number is a unique identification number that is assigned to a particular record created for each book in its cataloged collections. Librarians use it to locate a specific Library of Congress catalog record in the national databases and to order catalog cards from the Library of Congress or from commercial suppliers. The Library of Congress assigns this number while the book is being cataloged.*

On the copyright page of most books, you will see an LCCN. The number includes the year of publication and a unique serial number for each book title. Unlike the ISBN, the LCCN is assigned to the work itself, not to a particular media release. There is no fee from the Library of Congress for an LCCN.

## Preassigned Control Number (PCN)

It takes several weeks before the LOC issues a permanent LCCN. Not all books will be listed in the LOC. As a general rule, the LOC will not accept vanity published books.

A PCN is a pre-assigned control number and is issued by the Library of Congress temporarily, before the permanent LCCN may be issued. If you are a self-publisher or micro-publisher, you can apply for a PCN first. The pre-assigned control number or PCN must appear on the copyright page of your book when it goes to print.

## Apply

You can fill out a form online at **http://pcn.loc.gov/pcn.** When you see the screen that says Pre-assigned Control Number Program, click on **Open New Account**. (Figure 8.1) Once you have set up your new account, you must complete the Application to Participate form. (See Figure 8.2.)

When I registered this book online via my publishing company, DARBY PRESS, it took only six minutes for them to send me my pre-assigned control number!

**Figure 8.1**    Open New Account screen

This will bring up the next page; click on Application to Participate. The next screen will bring up the application itself. Fill out the information accurately.

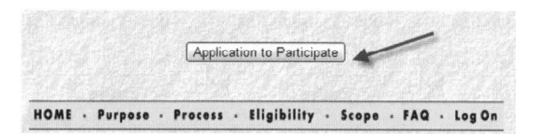

**Figure 8.2**        Application to Participate screen

Keep in mind that the Library of Congress does not accept vanity published books. If your book is written by Jane Smith and published by Jane Smith, you may be rejected on the grounds that it is a vanity published book.

### *Virgin's Note*

> *If you plan on marketing your book to libraries, you will need an LCCN. The best way to get one is to use the name of your publishing company on the Application to Participate form.*

The Library of Congress is looking for publishers, and publishers with several books in their catalog have a much better chance of being issued an LCCN (LCN). If you have set up your publishing company, your chances of obtaining this number are better. When the LOC receives your application, it will issue a pre-assigned number. Getting your PCN doesn't mean that you will be listed in the LOC. It can take weeks before your book is listed, if at all. The only way to know it has been listed is to check the LOC database periodically to see if it shows up.

***Virgin's Note***

*If you are applying for a pre-assigned control number through CreateSpace it takes approximately ten days to get your PLCN (Pre-assigned Library Control Number). To find out if your book has been permanently listed, you will have to check the LOC catalog periodically. This process can take several weeks.*

## Cataloging in Publication (CIP)

Cataloging in Publication (CIP) is a separate Library of Congress service. The CIP is a block of bibliographical data about your book. The Cataloging in Publication record (CIP data) is a bibliographic record prepared by the Library of Congress for a book that has not yet been published. On publication, the publisher includes the CIP data on the copyright page, thereby facilitating book processing for libraries and book dealers. The graphic below is a sample CIP.

Publisher's Cataloging in Publication data

Doe, Jane.
   Illustrating nature : environmental experiment / written and  illustrated by Jane Doe.
   p. cm.
   Includes index.
   ISBN 0-569519-08-9

1. Natural history illustration. 2. Scientific illustration. 3. Drawing -- Technique. 4. Nature (Aesthetics). I. Title.
HQ 46.5.B7 2004
508.022—cd12                              2014110033

**Figure 8.3**     Sample Catalog in Publication data block

As a new publisher, having this data block on your book's copyright page makes you seem larger than you are—that is a good thing. Here's the problem: to qualify for a CIP you need to have published three books. If you just started your publishing company and you haven't published three books, there is an alternative.

You can apply to Quality Books to become a distributor for your book.

Quality Books is a wholesale supplier to libraries. They will fill in for the Library of Congress with the Publisher's Cataloging in Publication or PCIP data blocks. The contact information for Quality Books is listed below.

Quality Books
1003 West Pines Road
Oregon, IL  61061-9680
(800) 323-4241 or (815) 732-4450
Fax (815) 732-4499
**http://quality-books.com**

## Categorizing Your Book

Most POD publishers will ask you to categorize your book. If you want to look at the categories that are available, you can go to:

***www.bisg.org/standards/bisac_subject/major_subjects.html***.

Properly classifying your book will help online retailers and potential readers find your book. Take a few moments to become familiar with these classifications. The better job you do here, the easier your readers will be able to find your book.

***Virgin's Note***

*During the CreateSpace author account set up, you will be asked to categorize your book. CreateSpace makes this process fairly easy. The categories are available in a dialogue box and can be easily selected. See Chapter 9 for more details.*

## Application Sequence

When I published my first self-published book, I was confused by all of the numbers. There is a specific sequence that works best. Item 1 should be done before your book is complete. Items 2, 3 and 4 can be done at or near completion. Items 5, 6 and 7 should be done when the book is completed, including editing.

1. Purchase your ISBN from **http://bowker.com** then **www.myidentifiers.com.**
2. Register your work with the Copyright Office at **http://copyright.gov.**
3. Register your book with the Library of Congress:

   Cataloging in Publication Division
   Library of Congress
   101 Independence Ave., S.E.
   Washington, DC  20540-4320
   (202) 707-6372

   (If you do this through CreateSpace, the cost is $75 and they will complete your application for a pre-assigned Library of Congress number or PCN.)
4. Enter your ISBN into CreateSpace.
5. Set up your book to be distributed through Quality Books.

Quality Books
1003 West Pines Road
Oregon, IL  61061-9680
(800) 323-4241 or (815) 732-4450
Fax: (815) 732-4499
**http://quality-books.com**

You apply to Quality Books if your publishing company has not yet published three books.

6.  Publish your book online with CreateSpace.
7.  Assign the ISBN in myidentifiers.com.

## OCLC-World Cat

World Cat is a global catalog with over 212 million bibliographic records that represent more than one billion individual items held by participating institutions. World Cat is used extensively by libraries internationally. World Cat is published in 470-plus languages and in over 112 countries. While it isn't mandatory that your book is entered into World Cat, it is helpful. If your book is listed in *Books In Print*[5] it may or may not be listed in World Cat.

Data about your book is precisely entered into World Cat by library staff. Some authors have had their books listed in World Cat by donating a copy or copies of their books to the library and asking the librarian to enter the book into World Cat. If libraries have requested your book, you may want to check with them to see if your book has been listed.

---

[5] Nearly all books, no matter the genre, may be listed in the World Cat database.

### *Self Publisher's Checklist*

✓ *Set up   the corporate structure of your publishing company including type of entity, principals of the business, name, address or post office box, and phone and contact information.*

✓ *Set up your account with Bowker.com.*

✓ *Order your ISBNs from www.myidentifiers.com.*

*"I admire anybody who has the guts to write at all."*

~E.B. White

# PART TWO

# WHAT YOU WILL LEARN IN THIS CHAPTER

How to create a
basic book layout
in Word

Interior layout
design principles
and physical set
up

Tools, fonts and
typefaces

Selecting trim
size and handling
graphics

# 9 INTERIOR LAYOUT

*"Writing is like prostitution. First you do it for love, and then for a few close friends, and then for money."* ~Moliere, French playwright, writer

Your manuscript is finished and has been professionally edited. Now you are ready to prepare your manuscript "layout." The layout is the interior design of your book. The layout relates to page headers and footers, trim size, chapter headings, fonts and type sizes, and sub-headings. If you are creating an index, glossary and/or appendices, then those, too, are part of your layout.

## Options

If you have never used any of the advanced features of Word, you can still create a professional layout using the instructions in this chapter. If you don't want to do your own interior layout, CreateSpace will prepare your book's interior layout for a fee.

There are two levels of interior layouts with CreateSpace:

Template driven                                    $299

(Layouts are templates created in Word and your file is loaded into the template.)

Custom Layouts                                        $499 and up

CreateSpace will create a custom layout for your book. These options take time and you will be working with a graphic designer. That means that the process can take six to eight weeks from start to finish. Make sure that you have allowed enough time in your publication schedule.

The first book I self published was for Women Who Write. The budget was practically non-existent, and forced me to become a student of self publishing. I read dozens of books on the subject, studied Web sites, and scoured Amazon to see what other self publishers were doing. When I talked to CreateSpace, they told me they used Word templates for basic interior layouts. I knew Word fairly well at the time, but I became a student of Word. In just a few days, I was proficient enough to do a credible interior layout.

## Publishing Software

There are several great programs on the market to create an interior book layout. These software applications, called desktop publishers, were created specifically for publishing. Adobe In Design CS5 (formerly PageMaker), Quark Express and Microsoft Publisher are all desktop publishing software and are capable of creating intricate interior book layouts, cover designs, flyers, brochures and more. If you plan on turning your book into an e-book you may want to consider using one of these programs. E-books, by their nature, need to have a more graphical and intricate user interface. These programs all have steep learning curves and are expensive. In Design and Quark cost several hundred dollars each.

I used Microsoft Word to create this book's interior layout. Word is readily available and is considerably less expensive than the programs listed above. When creating your book's interior layout with Word, it works best to set margins, gutters and paper size first.

## Versions

These instructions are written for Word 2007. You will find that if you are using Word 2003 or Word 2010 some of the menu names have been changed to protect the innocent. Don't worry; the names will be similar enough that you can easily convert the instructions to fit either version.

If your book is fiction, a memoir or other similar work, the interior layout, i.e., the design of the interior pages of text and/or graphics make up the interior layout. Up to now you have been concentrating on content, and concerned with spelling and grammar, flow, logical sequence and making it interesting to read. Now that you have an edited manuscript, it's time to see your text not as words, but as pages.  Put down your red editing pen and pick up your painting smock. Interior design requires the eye of an artist.

## Keys to Clean Interior Design

Listed below are what I consider to be the key elements of a clean interior design:

1.  Is the typeface easily readable?

2.  Is the spacing between lines or leading[6], headings and sub-headings appropriate and is the distance between paragraphs good?
3.  Are the tables or graphic elements clear and readable and consistently marked and labeled?
4.  Are the headers and footers consistent and aligned properly?
5.  Are the margins, gutter and white spaces all conducive to ease of reading?

## Typeface and Font Size

Choosing an appropriate typeface is a critical decision that should be made early in the process of writing your book. There are two basic types of fonts:

Serif fonts use short lines and curves, or embellishments called *serifs*. Serif fonts are popular in the United States and are good at guiding the reader's eye to the next character. This makes them a good choice for easy reading. The second type is sans serif. Sans serif fonts are plainer and don't have serifs.

Times New Roman is a serif font and if you look closely, you will see the serifs attached to each letter.

| Times New Roman | 12 pt. type | Serif |

Sans serif fonts use fewer embellishments. They work well with headings and sub-headings, but can be a bit

---

[6] Leading, pronounced *led´ ding*, comes from the practice of using metal strips (usually lead) of varying widths to separate lines of text in the days of metal type. In Word 2007. leading is controlled in the Paragraph section, via the Line Spacing icon.

harder on the eye when used for long passages of text.

Tahoma                                   12 pt. type          Sans Serif

As you can see from the sample above, fonts can vary greatly in the way they look. I used 12-point type for both typefaces, but the Tahoma font looks much larger.

Most books are written in 10- or 12-point type. Keep in mind, the point size you choose will have a huge impact on your page count. In a large book, point size can impact the cost of printing.

To review over 2,000 fonts, see **www.studio.adobe.com/us/type/main.jsp**. In general, stay away from fancy, curly or script-type fonts. These fonts are hard to read. Just as we strive to use simple words in writing so that we are easily understood, simple fonts also make the reading experience pleasant and fun.

Once you have selected a font, make sure it is available in **bold,** *italic* and in ***bold/italic***.

As a self-published author you need to select a font that is compatible with your POD printer.  Using the wrong font can result in special characters being misaligned with the rest of the text. The general rule for choosing a font or typeface is:

If your reader notices the typeface, then you have chosen poorly. *The typeface should always facilitate ease of reading, not distract from it.*

*Author's Note*

*Using the right typeface for your book is somewhat like the famous line from Coco Chanel, "Dress beautifully and they will notice the dress; dress impeccably and they will notice the woman."*

## Photos and Illustrations

If you are using photos and illustrations, it is important that they are placed in the body of your layout in a consistent and balanced way. Word does not lend itself well to a book with many graphic elements. It handles charts and tables better than photographs.

If you are writing a memoir or family history and need to include several photographs, use an insert in the middle of your book. Set aside several pages of photographs that can be viewed page by page. This will add interest to your memoir or family history, making the characters come to life, and it will be much easier to lay out in Word.

## Formatting

 Formatting includes page margins, page numbers, and running headers, as well as chapter headings and sub-headings. Remember, cluttered pages can be hard to read. The best way to keep your text from appearing crowded or hard to read is to adjust the distance between lines. Here is an example:

*This paragraph is written with the distance between lines set to 1. In a large book, this will become burdensome for the reader. It will fatigue the eye and make the text harder to read.*

*This paragraph is written with the distance between lines set to 1.15.  The greater distance between the lines makes the text easier to read.*

*This paragraph is written with the distance between lines set to 1.5.  This is easy to read, but over the long haul, may be a little too much distance between each line. Generally speaking, the more technical your information is, the more important it is to have a wider space between lines.*

## Trim Size

Trim size is the overall dimension of your book. If your book will be six inches wide and nine inches tall, the trim size is 6" x 9". Word refers to trim size as PAPER SIZE. In Word, your paper size and your trim size should be equal.

One of the keys to creating a professional looking layout for your book is to choose the correct trim size. Keep in mind that books produced with print-on-demand technology are soft cover, perfect bound books, not hard cover books. Find a softbound book on your book shelf that is the size you want to use for your book. Measure the book from the top edge, top to bottom, and then from the spine edge, side to side—this will be your trim size. Check the chart below to see which standard size measurement is nearest in size. Standard trim sizes are less expensive to print—using a standard trim size for your book will keep printing costs to a minimum.

The table below is a list of standard trim sizes for CreateSpace. For most books, the 6" x 9" trim size is adequate. If you are writing a technical book, a larger trim size might work better. It will allow the book to remain stable while lying on a desk in the open position. Listed below is a chart for standard trim sizes. Standard trim sizes will be less expensive to print and will look better on bookstore shelves.

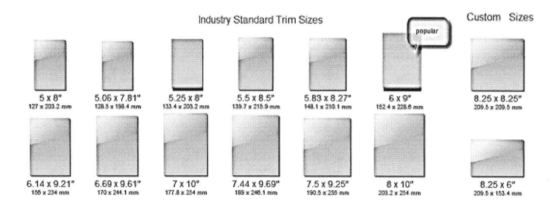

*Figure 9.1* – *Industry standard trim sizes*

If you are using Word as the application for creating your book, you should create the book in one file. Don't use different files for each chapter. Word is a word processor and not a publishing program. It works more efficiently as one file.

**Author's Note**

*When setting up the paper size in Word under PAGE LAYOUT make sure that the PAGE SIZE in Word matches the TRIM SIZE that you choose in Create Space .*

## Global Settings

Global settings are settings that impact the entire document. They are file attributes that will apply to all occurrences within your document. What are some global settings that you need to worry about? Margins and gutter size are global settings. Paragraph and sub-paragraph headings can be set up globally. Once you have decided what size your book will be, you can set the margins for your entire document.

In the example below, we are using a 6" x 9" layout.

## Setting Page Size

Now that you have decided on your trim size, it's time to set the margins for your book in Word. For this example, we are setting the margins for the entire document, or *globally*.

In Word, under the PAGE LAYOUT tab, select SIZE.
You will notice that there is no option to select a 6" x 9" layout. To select a size not listed, select MORE PAGE SIZES.
This will bring up a page called PAGE SETUP.
Select the PAPER tab.
Select WIDTH by using arrows to select 6."
Select HEIGHT by using the arrows to select 9."
Drop down the PREVIEW portion of the PAGE SETUP screen.
Select the "Apply To" box.
Select WHOLE DOCUMENT by selecting the arrowed scroll bar to right of the dialogue box.
Click OK.
You have successfully set your page size for your entire document.

## Setting the Margins

It's time to set up the margins. Your book has two types of margins: exterior margins which are the top, bottom and outer edge, and the interior margin, called the gutter.

## Gutter

The gutter is the space between the recto (right) and verso (left) pages of an open book.

Gutter

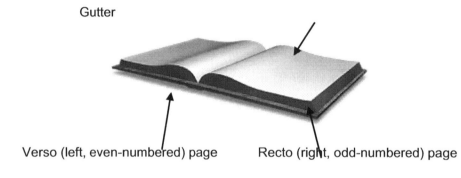

Verso (left, even-numbered) page          Recto (right, odd-numbered) page

**Figure 9.2**    Gutter illustration

In Word, your gutter setting will read .01. This will yield a properly sized gutter in your completed book. If you are writing a technical book and anticipate your reader may need more room for notes, you can increase this, but keep in mind that a small change here makes a big difference in the look and feel of your completed book.

**Now let's set the margins of your book:**

Go to the PAGE LAYOUT tab.
Select MARGINS, then select CUSTOM MARGINS.

Under the PAGE SETUP dialogue box, go to the MARGINS section of the dialogue box.
You will see TOP, INSIDE, GUTTER on the left side and BOTTOM and OUTSIDE on the right.
Change the TOP and INSIDE margins to the setting you want by clicking on the up and down arrows. (The margins for this book were set to 1.2.)[7]
Now set the margins for the BOTTOM and OUTSIDE on the right of the screen.
From the Pages section of the Page Setup/Margin screen, select MIRROR MARGINS.
From the PREVIEW section, select APPLY TO; choose WHOLE DOCUMENT.
Click OK.

Notice that the Word default value for the TOP, BOTTOM, INSIDE and OUTSIDE margins is usually one inch. This will work for most books. If you want smaller margins, you can take them down as low as a half-inch. Keep in mind, the smaller the inside and outside margins are, the harder your book will be to read. A page with small margins will always look more intimidating, and the longer lines will be harder to read. Margins of at least 1 to 1.2 inches work best.

MIRRORED MARGINS gives you the ability to insert page headers and/or footers and page numbers that are different on odd and even pages. This allows you to put the chapter name on the left page and the name of the book on the right page.

---

[7] Margins, or the distance the print stops from the outer edge of the page, will usually stay the same for an 8" x 10" trim size.

## Justified

You may want to justify all of the margins in your book. Justified text is even on both the right and left. Justified margins can make your book more difficult to read because the justification requires that some words in each line have more spacing between the letters than others. Many people feel that justified margins make the book look more uniform and professional. There is no right or wrong. This paragraph is left justified or "ragged right."

### Justified Sample Paragraph

When you are making interior layout decisions, use the books in your genre to decide what works. Inspect the margins, and the gutters of several books. What type of headers or footers did they use? How did they number the front matter—with page numbers or Roman numerals? Did they put page numbers at the bottom of the page and chapter titles at the top, or are both the chapter title and the page numbers in the header? These are design decisions that you will have to make. This paragraph has justified margins on the left and right.

One of the most important things you can do is be consistent with your choices throughout your entire book. To justify your text:

Select the HOME tab.

Go to the STYLES section of the task bar.
Select the box marked NORMAL.
Right click on NORMAL (if you see Heading 1, Heading 2...but not normal, use the scroll bar to the right to find NORMAL).
Right click, then select MODIFY.
In the FORMATING section of the dialogue box, click JUSTIFY icon.

## Chapter Headings

A good guideline to use when you are preparing your book's interior layout for publication is to begin each new chapter approximately one-third of the way down the page, from the top edge.

## Headers and Footers

If you plan on using an automatic table of contents in Word, it will be much easier to update if you use headings under the STYLE section of the HOME TAB in Word.

To set up headings for your document in Word:

SELECT the text you want as a chapter heading or sub-heading and highlight it.
Go to the HOME tab.
Go to the STYLES section of the HOME tab.
Select HEADING 2.
Right click on Heading 2.
Scroll down to MODIFY, then left mouse click.
In the Formatting Section of the MODIFY box, choose a font, point size, bold, italic, or color.
Click OK.
To set up a SUB-HEADING, choose HEADING 3 from the same STYLES section and choose your font and point size.

Setting up your headers in this way will ensure that they are uniform throughout your text.

## Running Headers and Footers

Take a book off the shelf and look at the header that runs across the top of the page, above the text. In most books, the left page header will have a page number on the left side of the page followed by the book title.

On the right page, the header will start with the chapter title, followed closely by the page number. These are the running headers and footers.

Here are some universal rules regarding headers and footers to keep in mind:

- The book title appears on one side of each page, and chapter titles appear on the facing page. The book title can appear on either the verso (left) or recto (right) page, but be consistent throughout the book.
- There is no header on the first page of a new chapter.
- Page numbers should be included in the header or in the footer.

## Section Breaks

In many books the front matter (introduction, preface and about the author) are numbered differently from the body of the book. If you have chosen to use headers or footers with the chapter title on one page, and book title on the facing page, you will need to insert a SECTION BREAK at the beginning of each new chapter. For the following example we are setting the right header as the book title, and the left header as the author's name. Don't forget, there are no page numbers or headers on the first page of a new chapter.

Position your cursor at the BEGINNING of the new chapter.

Go to PAGE LAYOUT.

Choose BREAKS, then, choose SECTION BREAKS.

Choose the option of starting a new section on the NEXT page.

Move your cursor to the start of the page where you wish your first header to appear.

Type INSERT, then HEADER, then EDIT. This will highlight the words LINK TO PREVIOUS. The LINK to PREVIOUS means you are NOT linking this header to a previous header, despite all intuitive knowledge to the contrary!

Click BLANK, then type your text.

Under OPTIONS, select DIFFERENT FIRST PAGE and DIFFERENT ODD and EVEN PAGES.

Now click PAGE NUMBERS.

Choose FORMAT page numbers.

Select format numbers, then select, START at page 1.

Type your header next to the page number.

Go to the first page of your chapter—if you see the words "TYPE TEXT" in the header section, delete the text.

Go to DESIGN.

Click CLOSE HEADER AND FOOTER.

To set up the header for the author's name, go to the first odd page of your book and repeat the process.

**Points to remember:**

> If you view your layout in Word two pages at a time, the pages will be reversed on your computer screen from the way they will appear in your finished book. Even pages will appear to be on the right of your screen and odd-numbered pages on the left. This is the opposite of what you will see in your printed book. It will help if you insert page numbers right away before you begin your layout.

## Adding a New Chapter

If you want headers with individual chapter titles, here is what you can do:

At the bottom of the page before your new chapter starts, select PAGE LAYOUT.
Select BREAKS and then click NEXT PAGE.
Go to INSERT HEADERS (or footers if you are using footers).
Select EDIT HEADERS—this will bring up the DESIGN MENU at the top of your screen.
Click LINK TO PREVIOUS (it sounds strange, but it tells Word that you do not wish to pick up the previous header).
INSERT page number, then type in your new chapter name, and CLOSE HEADER AND FOOTER.

## Ancillary Pages

If you plan on adding a bibliography, index or appendices to your book, you can choose to use the built-in commands in Word. The table of contents, endnotes, footnotes and index functions all work easily in Word 2007.

This chapter can be used to create a basic, professional layout. It will take time to understand the Word commands fully. Don't give up. In time you will become more proficient in Word.

**Author's Note**

*When preparing your headings and sub-headings, be sure your headings are consistent throughout your document. Make sure that all the headings use the same font, point size and spacing between the heading and its adjoining paragraph. A great layout is a consistent and uniform layout.*

**Self Publisher's Checklist**

- ✓ *Complete the manuscript.*
- ✓ *Finish the interior layout.*
- ✓ *Hire a book cover designer or contact CreateSpace to begin the process of designing a book cover. (You can also use the CreateSpace cover creator to build your cover.)*

# WHAT YOU WILL LEARN IN THIS CHAPTER

Book cover design basics

How people decide to buy a book

Seven rules to a great cover design

Integrating art work, photographs and graphics

# 10 BOOK COVERS THAT RULE

*"There is nothing to writing; all you do is sit down at the typewriter and open up a vein."*
        ~Walter Wellesley "Red" Smith

## Book Cover Basics

I know what you are thinking. My book cover is important, but not as important as what's inside—right? *Wrong.* Your book cover will sell your book. Most people really do judge a book by its cover. Make your cover count. There are two places where you should spent money on your book—*editing and cover design*.

According to Dunn-Associates, a book cover design firm (www.dunn-design.com), "a whopping 75 percent of booksellers say that the cover is the most important element of the book."

Book cover design is an art—don't try to do this yourself. CreateSpace has some excellent template designs that allow you to change the color or background pictures. You can customize the cover by using your text and photos. The cover templates are free. Custom designed covers start at $499.

If you are using a picture or a photograph, keep in mind that pictures, like words, can be copyrighted. Always obtain a release from the photographer, if necessary. If you are using the picture of a person, you should always get a signed release form.

### Author's Note

*There are enterprising people out there who buy up unsold, surplus copies of published books, change the cover art, re-market the titles and sell books by the truckload! What makes the difference? The cover!*

## How Book Buyers Buy

Before you decide on a cover, the first thing you need to know is how book buyers actually make the decision to buy a book. In today's market, there are two distinct types of buyers, and they choose the books they buy differently.

## Bookstore Buyers

When people go to the bookstore, they browse. The books that get the most scrutiny are those that are displayed facing out, where the entire front cover is exposed. These books are usually from writers of stature (best sellers and proven winners). Your first book won't be displayed facing out—it will be shelved in a bookcase. Think about it a minute, if your book is stored on a bookshelf alongside hundreds of other books; what is the most valuable piece of real estate on your book cover? *The spine.*

Your book cover design should always have a powerful, easy-to-read spine. Both the title and the author's name should be clear and readable by a person standing in front of the bookshelf. Go to your local bookstore and stand in front of several different bookshelves. Which titles seem to stand out? What colors did they use? Could you read the author's name and the title clearly? Was there a graphic element or a photograph on the spine? Make a note of the ones that caught your eye and figure out why.

According to most research, the average bookstore book buyer goes through a predictable pattern to find the book he or she wants:

- After browsing the front facing, prominently displayed books, they go to the bookcases in their genre's section.
- A buyer will spend approximately two to five seconds looking at the spines of books on the shelf.
- If he or she likes the spine or the title on the spine, they will pull it from the shelf, and spend an additional four seconds looking at the front cover.
- If your book is still a potential purchase, the potential buyer will look at the back cover where they will read your testimonials. If you have an author bio on the back page with a photograph, he or she will spend a few seconds on the bio.
- If your book is still in the running, the buyer will open the book and study the table of contents—for perhaps for twelve to fifteen seconds. They are looking to see if the information they want is in your book!
- If they like what they see, then you have made a sale!

## Online Book Buyer

Online buyers choose books differently. Since online buyers are usually in the comfort of their own homes or perhaps at the office when they make a purchase, they tend to spend just a little more time on the buying decision.

Online shopping, much like the bestseller rack at the local bookstore, shows all books facing out. Your entire front cover is visible to anyone who finds your book online! This is great for you as a self-published author because you now have the same real estate as Tom Clancy or Stephen King!

Remember, when buyers view your book online, the graphic will be small, so the book cover should be colorful and easy to read. The sub-title should explain the nature of your book.

Potential online buyers begin their buying process by typing in a search word. Buyers looking for *Self Publishing for Virgins* may type in "Create-Space " or "self publish" or "print-on-demand" to find it.

### Author's Note

*Always make sure that your sub-title explains what is in your book. When writing your sub-title, compile a search word list that closely describes the content of your book. Use words that potential buyers would be likely to use to search for your book. Amazon's search algorithm searches book titles first, and then it searches the sub-titles. Your sub-title is another opportunity to help buyers find your book.*

Once the buyer finds your book, they will quickly read the book description posted by Amazon. Some online buyers go directly to the "read what's inside this book" link. From there they will search the table of contents.

Spend an hour or two searching online for books that are similar to your book. Make a note of the search words you typed that gave the most targeted results. Observe what books show up under "suggested reading" in Amazon. These are clues to what will work for your book when it goes online.

### Author's Note

*Make your table of contents comprehensive. Online shoppers want to know that the information they seek is in your book BEFORE they buy it. How can they know that without skimming the entire book? By browsing a lengthy and comprehensive table of contents! Your TOC can sell your book!*

If your book is available through Amazon, and it will be if you are using CreateSpace.com, you will have to write a short blurb or synopsis of your book. You won't have a lot of room, but you can write a short paragraph. This paragraph should be the best sales pitch you can write. This is your chance to impress your reader and clearly communicate the function or story of your book. Take the time you need to write this description.

## Seven Rules to a Great Book Cover

1. One graphic element should establish a principle focus for the overall design. Don't put multiple graphic images on the cover. Too many elements will cause the eye to jump from object to object. Your book cover is like a billboard; it should be easy to read while going by at 60 miles per hour.
2. The graphics element you choose should convey something to the buyer about the nature of your book.
3. Don't use stark white backgrounds; they are hard to see online. Use shading or a subtle background design instead of pure white.
4. Make your title readable and large. View your cover in thumbnail size. This gives you an idea of how small it will look on Amazon's

site. If it is unreadable or seems cluttered in this small format, you need to simplify your design.

5. Keep your color palette simple. If you aren't comfortable with color choices, find a complementary color wheel online.
6. Go online or to the library and look at lots of great book covers. Examine which elements you like about each design. What fonts did they use? What type of graphic? What color choices did they make?
7. Browse the stock photo sites for graphics or photographs. Be sure the element or photograph you choose is not copyrighted or that you have obtained the proper licensing.

There are some great stock photo sites that you can use. Some are free and some charge a fee. Fees can range from a few cents to hundreds of dollars, so be sure that you are being given permission or a license with your purchase before using the graphic on your book cover. Here are a couple of sites with lots of stock photos.

**http://dreamstime.com**

**www.istockphotos.com**

## Creating a Compelling Back Cover

Don't forget that while the front cover gets the buyer hooked, the back cover reels them in. Here's what you need:

- Selling paragraph (a short paragraph at the top of the back cover; a quick, upbeat analysis of the benefits of buying and reading your book)
- Testimonials
- Book's list price
- ISBN

- Barcode
- Cover designer credit (only if you hired a designer)
- Publisher's name, address and logo (as a self-published author, you may or may not be the publisher. If not, leave this information out)

If you have obtained several high-profile testimonials, use them on the back cover and put your author bio in the back matter of your book. Along with the author bio, include a photograph. The photograph doesn't have to be a formal portrait, but it should be done professionally. A head shot is preferable. People like to know whose words they are reading. It's the first step to building a relationship with your readers.

## Selling Paragraph

What I call the "selling paragraph" is what most others call the book description. Don't take this lightly. The selling paragraph is usually a short five- or six-line description of your book which appears near the top of your back cover. It is your first and best opportunity to tell your buyer why they need your book. Tell the buyer about your book, but not too much. Focus the reader's attention on the benefits of reading your book.

## Testimonials or Blurbs

We all like to read what others have said about the book we are about to buy. So how do you get those coveted testimonials or blurbs? Prepare a form letter asking prominent people in your field to read the chapters and give you a short two- or three-line review.

If your book is non-fiction or a how-to book, include the first three chapters with your request. For fiction writers, you will need to send a copy of the entire book or galley copy. Most authors are very gracious and want to help. If your book is a hit and their name is on the back cover, they'll be happy to have given you the endorsement.

The best time to solicit testimonials or blurbs for your cover is three months before your publication date. This gives your readers plenty of time to respond. For more on getting blurbs and reviews, see Part Three.

## Author Bio

Your author bio is not a resume. It is biographical information about you that is relevant to your book. For the non-fiction writer, the reader wants to know the expertise and experience that you bring to writing the book. If your education is relevant or impressive, include it. If you are not the expert, but have interviewed experts, then include that experience. You could say, "John Doe has interviewed over 100 experts on this topic."

If your book is a memoir or romance, let the reader know how you came to write your book. This is sometimes referred to as your author's statement. If you have won any awards or have a university degree that is relevant to your subject, include that information.

Remember, this is an opportunity for your reader to get to know you better and to feel good about buying your book.  Your bio is a letter telling your reader why you wrote the book and what skills you brought to the table in order to write it. The bio should be no more than a paragraph long if it will appear on the back of your book. You should include a longer bio in the back matter of your book by using an *About the Author* page. As you write your bio, don't forget to include some personal information, hobbies, favorite books, favorite pastime and where you grew up—these things will build rapport with your reader. Include a professionally done headshot. Your picture doesn't have to be formal or stuffy, but it should be a clear, crisp, well-lighted image.

## ISBN-Barcode

The barcode (shown below) should appear on the lower right side of your back cover. As discussed earlier, the barcode makes it easy for retailers to inventory and sell your book. If you plan on selling your book online or in bookstores it must have a barcode and ISBN number. The book price will also become a part of the bar code.

**Figure 10.1**     Barcode sample

## Design Credit

If you have hired a graphic design firm or an individual to design your cover, then list that name at the bottom of the back cover. For example:

Cover design by *John Doe Designs,* **www.johndoedesgins.com**

## Summary

Once your cover design is done, stand back several feet and look at the cover. Can you see the main graphic element and tell what it is? Is the name of the book readable from a distance? Are the colors vibrant and eye-catching?

Look at the back cover. Does it look too cluttered? Is there too much text? Do the colors and use of white space look balanced? Are the fonts plain and easy to read?

Now check the spine. Have you taken the graphic element from the cover and put it on the spine? Can you clearly read the title and the author's name from a distance? Have you carried through the color scheme onto the spine?

If you are satisfied with the way your cover looks and feels, now it is time to take the most critical step of all—proofread your entire cover. Do it two or three times. Ask others to proofread it. The text must be perfect and free of typos.  With all of that done, you now have a wonderful book cover.

 *Self Publisher's Checklist*

✓ *Finalize your book title and sub-title.*
✓ *Save your book cover blurbs and author bio to a Word file.*
✓ *Check the Word file for spelling and grammar.*

*"No tears in the writer, no tears in the reader."*

~Robert Frost

# WHAT YOU WILL LEARN IN THIS CHAPTER

What is a PDF
file format?

Preparing your
pre-publication
file

Choosing the
right software

Converting your
Word
manuscript into
a PDF file

# 11 PRE-PUBLICATION FILE

*"Let's face it, writing is hell."*                    ~William Styron

## Pre-publication File

Once your book is written and professionally edited, it's time to prepare your Microsoft Word file for publication. While there are many types of output files that can be created, the most important file format for anyone in self publishing is the PDF file.

## PDF File Explained

PDF stands for Portable Document Format. PDF conversion programs convert all types of file formats into a universal, printable format called PDF. That means a PDF file can be printed by many platforms. Whether you have a Mac or a PC, both can read and print a PDF file. Since all PDF files conform to a standard and predictable format, they can be read by any computer that has access to a PDF reader. The best-known reader for PDF files is Adobe Acrobat. Most of us have a resident version of Adobe Acrobat Reader software on our desktops and use this reader for PDF files every day.

Print-on-demand printers, specifically CreateSpace, require your Word document to be converted to the PDF format before uploading. This saves the printer time and ensures that your file is in a format (PDF) that their high-speed digital printer will recognize. While Adobe Acrobat is the most popular PDF file conversion program out there, it is not the only one. You can get a free PDF program on the Web, but be careful. Not all PDF software is of the same quality. Acrobat is a very high-quality PDF converter and it comes with a price tag to show it. The cost of Adobe Acrobat on Amazon ranges from $184 for Acrobat Professional to over $400 for Acrobat Professional X.

The PDF conversion program featured in this book is Bluebeam PDF Revu. It retails for $99 and I have used it several times to create a PDF book file. I think that dollar for dollar Bluebeam PDF Revu is a good choice at an affordable price. Bluebeam also has a 30-day trial so you can try before you buy. To get your trial version, go to **www.bluebeam.com.**

## Converting Your Book File to PDF

1. Purchase a copy of Bluebeam PDF Revu, Standard Edition (available online at www.bluebeam.com) and install it.
2. Select FILE from the navigation bar.
3. Select CREATE PDF.
4. Open your Word document file in Bluebeam.
5. It will automatically convert your Word file to a PDF format.
6. Save the newly created PDF file to your desktop and exit the program.

You will need this file later after you have set up your account with Create Space . Keep it on your desktop or in your book directory, where you can quickly find it to upload to CreateSpace.

**Author's Note**

*The version of Microsoft Word you are using may have a Create PDF plug-in already installed. If it is an Adobe Acrobat plug-in, then use it. If it isn't, the quality of your PDF may not be good enough for publication.*

**Self Publisher's Checklist**

- ✓ *Obtain a quality PDF file conversion program like Bluebeam or Adobe.*
- ✓ *Create a PDF file from the original manuscript.*
- ✓ *Save it to your desktop.*

# WHAT YOU WILL LEARN IN THIS CHAPTER

Making your book available for sale on Amazon

Setting up your book on Create Space

Learn what to do BEFORE you setup your Create Space account

ISBN, LCCN and more

# 12 USING CREATESPACE

*"It's a damn good story. If you have any comments, write them on the back of a check!"*
~Earl Stanley Garner

## Preparing Your Word File

Setting up your author account in CreateSpace is easy if you take the time to prepare in advance. The best way to do this is to create a file in Microsoft Word and call it CreateSpace setup.doc. Save this file to your desktop so it will be easy to find when you begin your CreateSpace set up. Here is what you will have in your Word file by the end of this chapter:

1. Book title
2. Sub-title
3. ISBN number (if you have purchased your own)
4. A description of your book which is no more than 4,000 characters or an average of 730 words
5. Five key search words or phrases
6. Retail book price
7. Discounts that you want to give to groups of individuals who buy your book

8. Blurbs or testimonials for the back cover
9. Book description for the back cover that is approximately one or two paragraphs (length may vary according to your cover design)

## Search Words

Finding just the right search words for your book is important. Key search words are actually meta-data and will be used to help online book sellers to properly categorize your book. One way to find some great search words is to pick five or six books that are strong sellers in the same genre as your book. Take each title, one at a time, and search for them on Amazon using various search words.

When I typed in the word "Christian" in the Amazon search bar, this is the information that I got back:

**Figure 12.1**                "Christian" tag results

This day there were 5,380 products in Amazon tagged "Christian."[8]

You can also see on the left, some of the other Christian classifications on Amazon. Discover more about search words in Section Three.

---

[8] This information is found under the search bar on Amazon.

## What to include in your book description

Have you ever read a book jacket in the book store? Think of your book description as your online book jacket and write it accordingly. If your book is fiction, tell a little bit about your characters and talk about the obstacles they encounter, but don't say too much or give away the plot! If you aren't sure what to write, go to Amazon.com and read several descriptions of books in your genre. Pick out two or three that you like and model your book description after those.

- Focus on the book itself, but you may also include references to other comparable books and/or authors.

Some things to remember:

- Books sold through CreateSpace will also have a detail page on Amazon.com.
- Once your book is approved and available for sale you can change the book description, keywords, BISAC category and list price. This information can be updated through your CreateSpace account.
- If you opted for the CreateSpace Expanded Channel Distribution (which you should), your book's description displays on all sales channels you choose.

BISAC stands for Book Industry Standards and Communications. It constitutes the main standards forum of the Book Industry Study Group. This group studies trends in publishing and sets categorization standards for the book industry.

**CreateSpace Content Restrictions**

CreateSpace does have content restrictions. The key restrictions are:

- Pornographic, obscene or offensive content
- Phone numbers, physical mail addresses, e-mail addresses, or Web site URLs.
- Links to other Web sites for placing orders or alternative shipping offers
- Spoilers (information that reveals plot elements crucial to the suspense, mystery or surprise ending of a story)
- Solicitations for positive customer reviews
- Advertisements, promotional material, or watermarks on images, photos or videos
- Time-sensitive information

## Getting Started with CreateSpace

If you have listed your title, sub-title, book description and other information in your Word document file and stored it on the desktop, you are ready to begin.

This step-by-step process takes you from opening your CreateSpace account, to uploading your book, creating a cover design, setting up Expanded Distribution and publishing your book on Amazon.
The sections below follow the entry screens in the CreateSpace set-up program as they appear. Go to **createspace.com** on your browser:

## Select AUTHORS

**Figure 12.1**    CreateSpace  new account screen

Next choose "CREATE NEW ACCOUNT" by clicking on the box marked **Sign Up Now**.

**Figure 12.2**    CreateSpace new account screen

## Creating Your Account

### Type in **www.createspace.com**

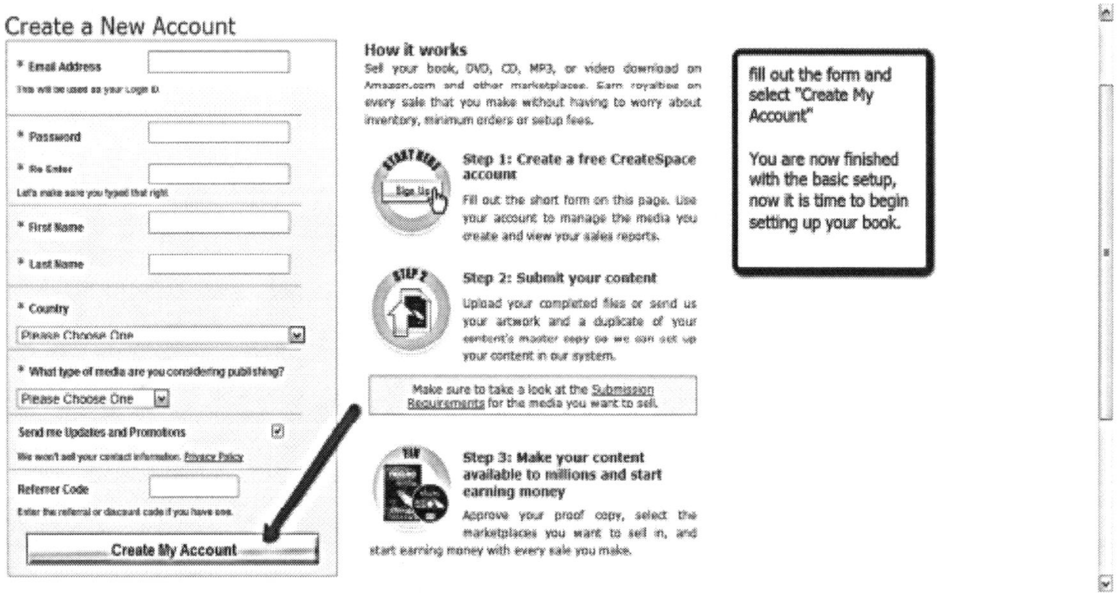

**Figure 12.3**    CreateSpace new account screen

Enter the following information:

- E-mail address
- Password
- Re-enter password
- First name
- Last name
- Country
- Media (choose book)
- Check SEND ME UPDATES
- Click on CREATE MY ACCOUNT

Always use an active email address. Enter a password; make it something easy to for you to remember, but not easy for someone else to guess. Once you have entered the email address and password, write them down and keep them some place safe.

Congratulations; you have an author's account in CreateSpace!

Now that the account is established, it is time to enter the technical details of your book. Let's take it one step at a time. Exit CreateSpace and log back in using your new password and user ID. If all goes well and you have entered the correct information, then you will see the screen below.

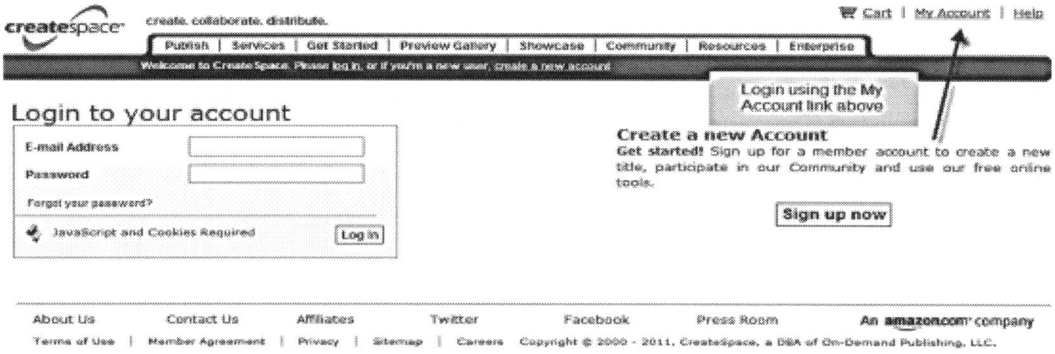

**Figure 12.4**     CreateSpace login page

## Setting Up Your Book

Once you have correctly entered your password and email address, you will see a new screen called *Member Dashboard.*

*Member Dashboard* is the central hub of your CreateSpace account. This is where you enter a new title (the name of your book), get reports, retrieve email messages, talk with the community of CreateSpace authors or edit your account settings. Here are the options on your *Member Dashboard* with a brief explanation of each:

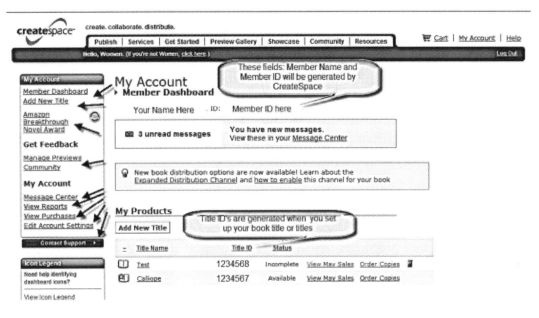

**Figure 12.5**        CreateSpace member dashboard page

- **Add New Title**—Set up the parameters for your newest book.
- **Amazon Breakthrough Novel Award**—If your book is fiction, you may want to enter it into Amazon's Breakthrough Book Award. If you wish to enter your book, press this link and CreateSpace will walk you through how to enter. You use this link only *after* you have published your book.
- **Manage Previews**—Allows you to make a part or your entire book available for preview to the CreateSpace community at large with a Public Preview, or to a select group of people using a Private Preview. Those who read your book or book excerpt will be able to write a review. These reviews are then available to you through CreateSpace.
- **Community Link**—With this link you can join the CreateSpace community forum and participate or read discussions of topics of interest to self publishers using CreateSpace.

- **Message** Center—Retrieve email messages. All messages sent to you from CreateSpace will also be copied to the email account you used to set up your account.
- **View Reports**—View sales reports which include sales both on CreateSpace and Amazon.com.
- **View Purchases**—View purchases of author copies.
- **Edit Account Settings**—Enter new mailing addresses, bank accounts, discounts.

To set up a new title, simply press ADD NEW TITLE, located in the middle of the Member Dashboard Screen.

## Start New Title Project

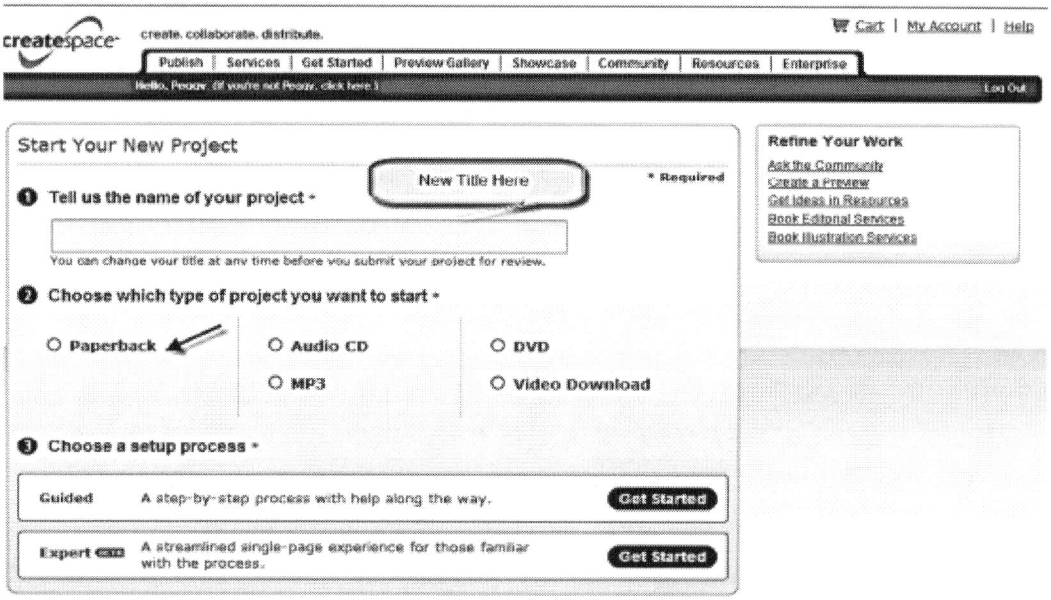

**Figure 12.6**    CreateSpace new project page

Take a deep breath and click ADD NEW TITLE. This is where you will add the title and sub-title of your book. Let's take this screen item by item.

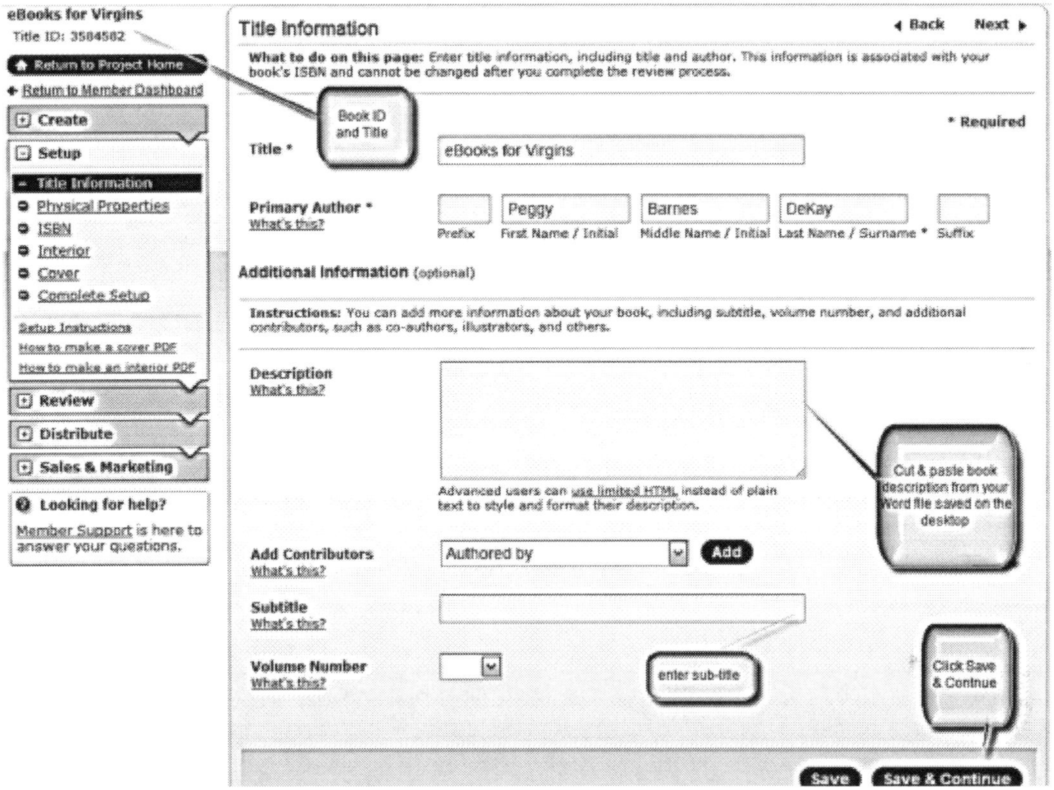

**Figure 12.7**          CreateSpace title information page

1. **Title**—Enter the title of your book. Be sure that the title is exactly as it appears in your copyright information.

2. **Primary Author**—Enter your name or pseudonym here. If you are using a middle name on the copyright page of your book, this field should be identical. All documentation, sales literature,

press releases or other marketing media should use the same name as your copyright registration form.

3. **Book Description**—You should have already written the book description and saved it to your Microsoft Word CreateSpace set-up document. Now all you have to do is pull up your Word document, select the text for your book description, right click your mouse, then hit COPY from the pop-up menu. Move your mouse pointer to the description block in CreateSpace, right click again, then select Paste. This copies the description into the CreateSpace description block. The description displays on your CreateSpace landing page.

4. **Add Contributors**—CreateSpace will allow you to add up to 20 contributors (20 contributors includes the primary author). A good example of using contributors is an anthology where there are likely to be several contributors. When using the contributors option, remember that Amazon truncates most of this information so it will not appear on the Amazon sales page.

5. **Sub-Title**—Enter the sub-title here. If you completed and assigned your ISBN form and the PCN form, be sure the sub-title and author names are identical on all forms. Make sure that you have no spelling errors and that the wording is correct. If you have saved your sub-title to your prep document, then cut and paste as before. Remember that you want to have a fairly long sub-title for Amazon.com, especially if your book is non-fiction. Make sure that the sub-title incorporates some of the key search words that your buyers will use to search for your book. This seems quite long, and it is, but look at the number of search words.

6. **Volume**—The volume number is for books published in series. Some anthologies that are published each year have volume numbers.

## Physical Properties Page

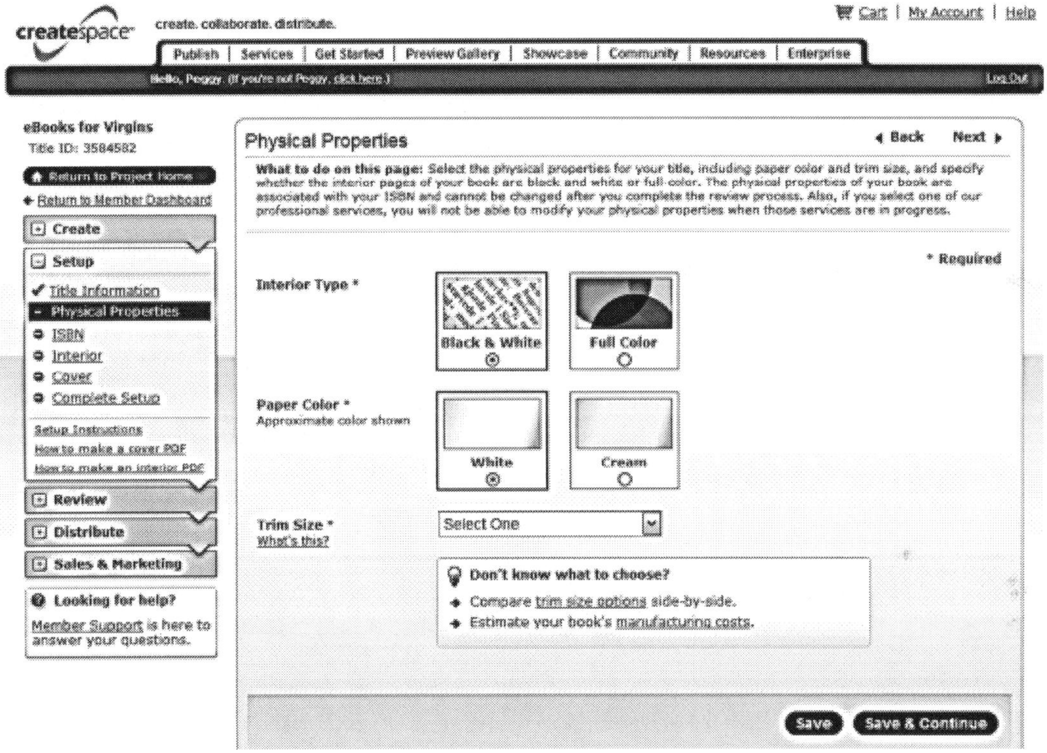

**Figure 12.8**    CreateSpace physical properties page

The physical properties page will help you select the trim size and interior color.

1. **Interior Type**—Here you will select either black and white or full color. If you are doing a children's book or a reference or

photography book that requires color pictures, then choose full color.

2. **Black and White**—If you are writing a memoir, self-help, how-to or fiction book, choose black and white.

3. **Trim Size**—The trim size is the size of your printed book. The first number is always the width and the second is the height. Listed below are industry standard trim sizes. If you plan to market your book through the CreateSpace Expanded Channel, you must choose an industry standard trim size.

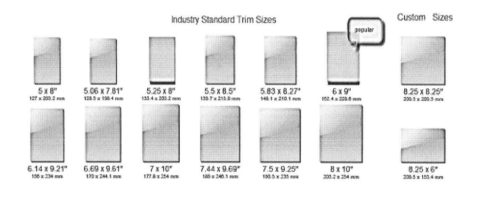

**Figure 12.9**    CreateSpace standard trim sizes

  **Author's Note**

*Remember, interior color is still pricey for most print-on-demand printers. While this is changing rapidly, you should be aware that printing a children's book of 32 pages may have the same production costs per book as printing a 200-page black and white, non-fiction book.*

## ISBN Page

Under *Provide Your Own ISBN,* you are asked to also provide the name of the imprint associated with your ISBN. This is the name of your publishing company. My publishing company is DARBY PRESS, LLC. That means that my "imprint" is DARBY PRESS, LLC. If you have not purchased an individual ISBN number, then you will need to select the first option, "Free CreateSpace Assigned ISBN."

**eBooks for Virgins**
Title ID: 3584582

★ Return to Project Home
◆ Return to Member Dashboard

▣ Create
▣ Setup
✔ Title Information
✔ Physical Properties
▪ ISBN
● Interior
● Cover
● Complete Setup

Setup Instructions
How to make a cover PDF
How to make an interior PDF

▣ Review
▣ Distribute
▣ Sales & Marketing

❷ Looking for help?
Member Support is here to answer your questions.

**ISBN**          ◀ Back    Next ▶

**What to do on this page:** An ISBN is required to publish and distribute a book. Compare ISBN options and find the one that's right for you.

* You can skip this section if you haven't decided which ISBN option to use, but you'll need to complete this page before you can publish your book. Return to your Project Homepage

**Choose an ISBN option for your book:**

○ **Free CreateSpace-Assigned ISBN**
We can assign an ISBN to your book at no charge.

○ **Custom ISBN**                    Only $10
Set your own imprint to be listed as the publisher.

○ **Custom Universal ISBN**          Only $99
Set a custom imprint while keeping your distribution and publishing options open.

○ **Provide Your Own ISBN**
If you have an ISBN that you purchased from Bowker® or through your local ISBN agency, you can use it to publish your book through CreateSpace. You must also enter the imprint name associated with the ISBN.

Read what authors in our Community say about selecting an ISBN for your book.

**What's the difference between an ISBN and an LCCN?**
• An ISBN is used by bookstores, retailers, and libraries identify books.
• An LCCN is an optional number that the Library of Congress assigns and uses for cataloging and other book-processing activities. An LCCN can only be assigned to books that have not been previously published.

Learn about obtaining an LCCN for your book.

**Figure 12.10**       CreateSpace ISBN page

The ISBN page will give you four CreateSpace options for your ISBN.

| CreateSpace ISBN Services Offered | Fee | Publisher of Record Status |
|---|---|---|
| 1.  Free CreateSpace Assigned ISBN | Free | Publisher of Record will be CreateSpace. |
| 2.  Custom ISBN | $10 | CreateSpace provides the ISBN, but will use your imprint name. |
| 3.  Custom Universal ISBN | $99 | CreateSpace will purchase the ISBN number while keeping your distributor options open. |
| 4.  Provide your own ISBN | $125 each for individual author or a block of 10 ISBNs is $250 for a publishing company | You purchase your ISBNs independently of CreateSpace at Bowker.com. |

**Table 12.11**        Charges for ISBN options

**Option 4: Provide your own ISBN** – If you choose this option; you should have already purchased your ISBNs. This option means that you or your publishing company will be listed in all databases, including *Books In Print,* as the publisher of record.

## Assigning an ISBN

If you chose option four, then you have purchased your own ISBN. When you are ready to publish your book and set it up in CreateSpace you will have to assign your ISBN to your book. This is done at **http://myidentifier.com.** Once the ISBN is assigned to your book, it cannot be re-used. Before entering your ISBN into CreateSpace, you should assign it first. If you later decide to publish your book as an e-book or an audio book, you will need a different ISBN for each media type.

## Imprint Name

Once your ISBN has been assigned, CreateSpace will ask you to enter your ISBN number and your imprint name. Your imprint name is your publishing company name. Be sure that you list the name exactly as it appears on myidentifier.com. If you purchased only one ISBN in your name, then your imprint name is your name.

***Author's Note***

*ISBNs are expensive. If purchased one at a time, the cost is $125 each. Bowker.com offers publishers discounts on blocks of 10, 250 and 1000 ISBNs. If you don't have or haven't started your own publishing company, you will not be eligible for discounts on ISBNs from Bowker. If CreateSpace supplies your ISBN, then CreateSpace will be listed in Books In Print as the publisher of record.*

## myidentifiers.com

The Web site **myidentifiers.com** is a Bowker Web site. This is where Bowker will send you to purchase your ISBNs. From myidentifyers.com you can manage identifier services for your ISBN as well as your publisher information. You will need to create an identifiers account if you haven't already. Your book's information, including title, author and physical properties will automatically populate your myidentifiers.com account within a few days of making your book available.

## LCCN

CreateSpace will help you obtain your Library of Congress Number (LCCN, sometimes referred to as LCN). The LOC does not charge authors or publishers to issue a number. CreateSpace, however, will charge you $75 to make application to the Library of Congress on your behalf. It takes approximately ten business days to receive your pre-assigned LCCN from CreateSpace. To be considered for cataloging in the Library of Congress database, one copy of your book must be submitted to the Library of Congress. If you have paid the $75 fee, CreateSpace will handle the application process for you.

If you have elected to be your own publisher, you will have to complete the application and send the Library of Congress a review copy of your book. You must follow through and send the LOC a copy of your published book; failure to do so can keep your book from being listed.

Making application for inclusion in the Library of Congress does not guarantee that your book will be accepted. The Library of Congress doesn't notify you regarding its acceptance or rejection of your book. To find out if your book has been cataloged, check the catalog at **www.loc.gov/index.html.**

An LCCN can only be assigned to books that have not been previously published. Once you approve your proof, your book is no longer eligible to begin this service.

**Author's Note**

*As discussed in Chapter 8, having a pre-assigned LCN or LCCN on your copyright page will help you market your book to the library system. Enrolling in the Create-Space Expanded Channel enrolls your book with Baker & Taylor and Ingram Books. Baker & Taylor sells books to the library market. Learn more about marketing to libraries in later chapters.*

## Interior Layout Page

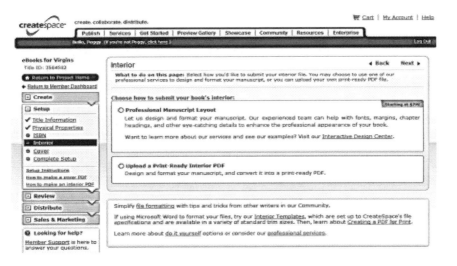

**Table 12.12**   Interior layout options page

Here you can choose to upload a PDF version of your book or you can let CreateSpace prepare your interior layout for you.

1. **Professional Layout by Create Space** – CreateSpace will prepare your interior layout for you. A basic template design starts at $299. For more intricate interior layouts, the fees are higher.

2.  **Upload Print-Ready PDF** – Choose this option if you have already created your interior layout and then converted the document to a PDF.

## CreateSpace Cover Templates

You can pick a layout from pre-designed templates. You can customize templates by changing background colors and background pictures. You can add your text to the front, back and spine of your book. Most of the templates for books over 100 pages will have printed spines. Books that are smaller than 100 pages are not thick enough to have printed spines.

CreateSpace has made it easier to design your own cover by adding lots of background photos that are inter-changeable with layout templates. Most templates will have an area for the author's photo (this image should be at least 300 dpi).

If you have hired a graphic designer, you simply need to press the upload button and uncheck the box marked "visible." Upload your book cover, making sure that the book cover and the trim size are the same.

If you are using a CreateSpace template for your cover, don't be afraid to change colors and background photos. This part of the site is WYSIWYG, which means "what you see is what you get." You will see how the finished cover will look instantly. As you change colors and backgrounds, the screen will adjust accordingly. Always do a final proof of all the text on your book cover.

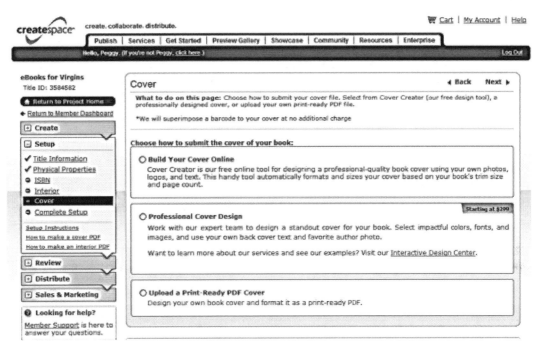

**Table 12.13**                  Cover options page

If you have chosen to create your own cover, then select Build Your
Cover Online.

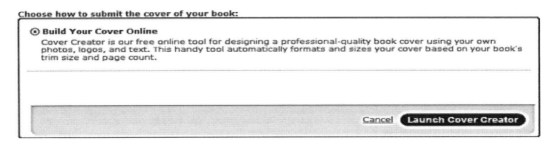

**Table 12.14**                  Launching cover creator

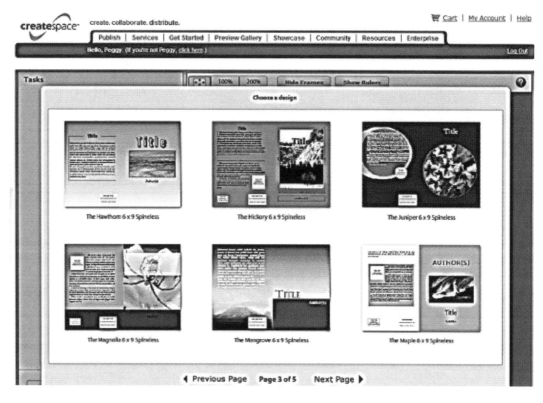

**Table 12.15**                Cover options

The covers above are samples of "spineless" covers. What does this mean? If your book is less than 100 pages, the spine will not be thick enough to be printed. If your book is more than 100 pages, CreateSpace will give you more options for covers with spines.

## Author's Bio

Your author's biography should also be pre-written and saved in a section of your CreateSpace set-up Word document. Remember, the author bio is not a résumé, but more a writer's statement. Ask yourself these questions:

- How did I come to write this book?
- Why I am uniquely qualified to write it?
- What are the experiences, degrees or achievements that helped me to write about this subject?

## Search Words

CreateSpace will allow you to enter five search words or phrases into their program. Choose these words carefully because they are the key words that will classify your book with Amazon.com. These five words or phrases should be chosen before you set up your account.

Here is an example:

Jane Smith is a Kentucky poet and she has written a book of poetry about living in the South. The search words she might choose would be— *poems, poetry, southern poetry, poetry collections, and Kentucky poets.*

### *Author's Note*

*When determining what to use as your search words, you can use keywords by Google to find out how many people are searching the Internet using the search word or phrase you type in. If your book is about flying, and you search on aviation, airplanes and aeronautics and you see that "aeronautics" is used the least, then eliminate it and find another word with a higher ranking. Google's keyword search is a part of Adsense and you will have to sign up for a free trial. You can use* **www.submitexpress.com/keytracker.php** *to test 15 words or phrases for free. It gives you a nice comparison between Summit Express and WordTracker results.*

## Book Price

Your book price is the retail price of your book. It should be five to eight times the cost of production plus fulfillment. Calculate your book price and enter it here. (Fulfillment is the cost of getting author copies to you—calculate the average cost per book to have books shipped to your door.)

## Trim Size

Most non-fiction books are printed in the 6" x 9" size. Many how-to books like this one are printed in a larger format for easier reading and to accommodate graphics. This book is printed in the 7.5" x 9.25" format.

The two trim options under "Custom" make great formats for children's books and specialty books. If you are selling a humor book for the gift store market, one of these custom sizes may be just right for you.

Last year I did two books on CreateSpace , a cookbook and an anthology. The cookbook was done in the 8.25" x 8.25" format and the cost of printing was $2.15. The book was 79 pages. The second book, an anthology, was a 6" x 9" and 179 pages. The printing cost per book was $3.15.

## Categories

The next screen (shown below) allows you to choose categories for your book. Take a moment here to study the categories and sub-categories. It is important that you categorize your book correctly because it will help people find it.

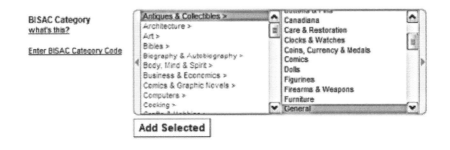

**Table 12.16**        Book categories

# BISAC Category

What is a BISAC category? BISAC stands for Book Industry Standards and Communications. It constitutes the main standards forum of the Book Industry Study Group. BISG's Digital Standards Committee develop industry-wide digital publishing standards and best practices that support the production, distribution, marketing, sale, discovery and use of books in digital form.

Try to get the best possible match in both the overall category and the sub-category. The better job you do here, the easier you will make it for people to find your book!

# CreateSpace Landing Page

Now that you have entered all of your data, uploaded your book, and uploaded or created your cover design, it is time to build your landing page with CreateSpace.

Here's how it works: When you use CreateSpace to publish your book, they give you two selling sites with two different commissions (we will talk about commissions later). The first site is your Amazon.com listing and the second is your CreateSpace landing page.

Do you remember the description that you prepared for your book? This will become part of your sales page on CreateSpace. Make this book description count—make it compelling so that people will be intrigued and want to buy your book.

## Using Your Web Site Banner

You will notice that CreateSpace gives you the option to enter a title URL. If you have a Web site with your logo or book logo across the top of the web page and you would like to use it in your CreateSpace landing page, position your cursor over the banner on your site, right click your mouse and notice the address in the browser. Select the entire browser address with your mouse, right click and copy the address. Return to your CreateSpace page and paste the URL into the page where indicated.

When you go to your CreateSpace landing page, you will see your Web site banner at the top of the page! This is a great marketing tool and it is easy to do.

## Expanded Distribution Channel

The expanded channel option is only available to those who have purchased the Pro Plan. The CreateSpace Pro Plan costs a one-time fee of $39. It's well worth the money. Choose "yes" when asked if you want to participate in the Pro Plan for your title. The Expanded Channel option also enrolls your book in the databases of Ingram Books and Baker & Taylor. These distributors will, in turn, have your book listed in their databases which are accessed by libraries, bookstores and other retail outlets.[9]

---

[9] Caution: only books using a standard trim size will be eligible for all distributed channels.

## Getting a Proof

Once you have completed all of the steps to set up your book, you are ready to order a proof. After you have uploaded your interior PDF file to Create Space, they will check your file for content. This process takes a day or two. Once their check is complete, you will receive an email from CreateSpace asking you to order a proof.

Your proof can be ordered online, through your author account. It will take two to five business days to arrive, depending on the shipping option you choose. The cost of a proof is the same as the cost of an author copy, but shipping can be more expensive. Plan on spending $20 to $30 to have five proof copies sent second-day air. You can order up to five proofs, but no more. The proof will be an *exact copy* of your book. Check it carefully before approving it!

Once your proof arrives, let your editor (I hope you hired one) look over the proof one last time. He or she will be looking for typos, spacing issues, widows and orphans[10], consistency in chapter headings, and sub-headings, and mistakes in the table of contents. If you have appendices or an index, she may want to check those as well.

## Making Changes to a Proof

If your editor finds mistakes, they can be corrected. Make the required changes to your original final draft in Microsoft Word. Once that is done, reload your corrected Word document into Bluebeam and create a new PDF.

---

[10] Widows and orphans—widows are lines left alone at the top of the page, separated from the rest of the paragraph. Orphans are lines left alone at the bottom of the page. Use the widows and orphans function in Word to eliminate these.

Log on to your CreateSpace account and upload your new PDF interior file. The process of uploading a new PDF will erase the old file automatically. When the new PDF is uploaded, CreateSpace repeats the process of approving content, and requests that you order a second round of proofs. This takes time, so don't crowd your publication schedule.  Each round of corrections will take approximately five to seven business days to complete. It makes sense and saves time to get it right the first time.

If you and your editor are satisfied with the results, then select "approve your proof." Once your proof is approved, your book will be published online at Amazon.com and on your CreateSpace.com landing page. It takes about two days for the published book to be linked with the landing page and to be uploaded with a sales page on Amazon. CreateSpace will send you a link to your landing page.

It's that simple—you are a published author!

In only a matter of days you have gone from a finished manuscript to a published book. Congratulations!

## CreateSpace Commissions

As of this writing, CreateSpace takes a 20 percent commission from each book sale originating from the book landing page at CreateSpace. If your book is sold on Amazon, their commission is 40 percent. Commissions are calculated on the list price of your book regardless of printing costs.

## Ordering Author Copies

Author copies are the books you buy directly from CreateSpace at cost. You should have 50 to 100 books on hand at all times. CreateSpace has good pricing on author copies. As a self-published author, you will sell many of your books out of the trunk of your car, from the back of a room during a sales presentation or at training seminars. In order to maximize your profits on these sales, you must be able to purchase author copies for less than 30 percent of the retail price of your book. Books of 200 to 250 pages, in black and white, should cost the author less than four dollars each.

CreateSpace allows authors to make a profit when ordering author copies. Since Amazon is interested in providing as many niche books as possible to the largest number of book buyers, they don't charge them a premium price for author copies.

## Pro Plan

During the set-up process, CreateSpace will ask if you want to upgrade your author's account to the Pro Package. The cost for the upgrade is a one-time fee of $39. I strongly suggest that you spend the money. The Pro Package gives you a significant discount on the wholesale price that you pay for author copies.  Keeping your author copy cost low allows you make more profit each time to do a direct sale.

### *Self Publisher's Checklist*

- ✓ *Enter the title and sub-title.*
- ✓ *Assign an ISBN if applicable.*
- ✓ *Enter the ISBN number into CreateSpace.*
- ✓ *Enter the imprint (publisher) name, if applicable.*
- ✓ *Cut and paste the book description from the Word doc into CreateSpace.*
- ✓ *Request a pre-assigned LCCN application or order from CreateSpace.*
- ✓ *Enter a trim size.*

✓ *Create a cover design from a template or upload a design to CreateSpace.*
✓ *Determine the list price of your book.*
✓ *Upload your interior book file in PDF format to CreateSpace. If CreateSpace is doing the interior layout, upload the edited Word file.*
✓ *Order a proof.*
✓ *Approve the proof when it arrives.*
✓ *Link the CreateSpace landing page to your Web site then celebrate briefly.*
✓ *Read Part Three of* Self Publishing for Virgins.

# PART THREE

# WHAT YOU WILL LEARN IN THIS CHAPTER

Author bio and
media kit

Golden rules of
self published
authors

Buying author
copies

Building your
lists

# 13 TAKE YOUR BOOK TO MARKET

*"A man walks into a bookstore. 'Where's the self-help section?' he asks the clerk. She shrugs and replies, 'If I tell you, won't that defeat the purpose?'"*
~Anonymous

There are many ways to make money from your self-published book. Your only limitation is your own imagination. In this section, we will talk about the different ways that, as a self-published author, you can sell your book. You will learn how to make the most of your book's listing on Amazon.com using your Author Profile. Then we will cover some of the "stealth" or unconventional ways that other self-published authors have been able to market their books.

First, let's talk money. Why? Because the first rule of business is *you have to make money*. "But I am a wordsmith," you may say, "the sensei of sentences, the guru of grammar, the master of metaphor." You may be all those things and more, but once your book is published, you are the CEO of your business!

## Making the Money Work

You may hate math, but it's time to get down and dirty and talk about the numbers. We need to talk about author copies. When your book is published, you will sell many of your books online, in bookstores and at book fairs, but many books will also be sold by you, personally. I call these trunk sales. You might sell books in the back of the room (called

BOR, or back-of-room sales) after giving a workshop, out of the trunk of your car, or after a book signing. You may sell your books to corporations by offering them a steep discount on bulk purchases. Wherever you have trunk sales, these will be the books that you have purchased yourself—author copies.

Many self-publishing sites charge premium pricing, as much as 50 percent of the retail price of the book for author copies. If you are thinking of having one of these self-publishing sites print your book—rethink it!

Let's say my book retails for $20. My POD sells me my own books for 50 percent off or $10. That sounds great, doesn't it? But think about it. When I approach an independent book store to sell my books, they will want a minimum of 40 percent off the list price. On top of that, because they are working with an author directly, instead of a wholesaler, they may want 45 to 50 percent off the list price. At 45 percent off the list price, I will have to sell my $20 book to the indie (independent) book store for $12. But how can I do that when I am paying $10 plus shipping, per copy? Do you see how quickly the profit can go away?

## The Golden Rules of POD

As I have discussed before, you are not just an author, you are a business owner. Your book is your business. Your publishing company is your business. Your speaking engagements as a result of your book are your business.  As a 30-year plus entrepreneur, here are my seven golden rules of business for authors.

## Seven Golden Rules for Authors

1.   The first rule of business is—you've got to make money.

2.  Pay yourself first!
3.  The retail price of your book should be no less than five to eight times the total cost of production plus fulfillment (shipping costs).
4.  Never deal with a POD that asks for more than 30 percent of the retail price of the book for author copies.
5.  Never deal with a POD that dictates the retail price of your book.
6.  Never use a POD that requires a minimum order of books.
7.  Always have author copies on hand—*always.*

Now that you have the numbers down, let's move on to building the solid foundation you need to establish yourself as an author, expert and speaker.

## Author's Bio

Your author's bio is really a sales letter to your potential readers. Many of your readers will be curious about how you came to write your book and they will want to know why you are qualified to write it.

When you are ready to do press releases and personal appearances, you will need a knock-out author bio. Don't write your author bio for yourself; write it for your reader. Pretend you have just purchased your book and are opening it for the first time. You begin to read the author's bio. What is it you would want to know about the author? Put that information in your bio.

Don't forget to include a few personal things. If you like to ride bikes or you're an ace Scrabble™ player, then share that information. Why? I can't tell you how many times people have hired me as a publishing consultant because of something they read about me that they can identify with. Why not tell them your hometown, or the state in which you were born? Your readers want to identify with you. If they feel they have something in common with you—all the better.

Here are seven questions that you will need to answer in order to write a great bio.

## Seven Keys to a Great Author Bio

1. What does my reader *need* to know about me?
2. If I were reading my book, what would I want to know about the author?
3. Why am I qualified to write this book?
4. How did I come to write the book—what is my "back story?"
5. What benefit will my reader get from reading my book?
6. Have I given the reader a little bit of personal information?
7. Have I shared the benefits of reading my book with the reader?

The reader wants to know how you came to write the book, and why you are qualified (either through education, or a unique experience or through extensive interviews with experts). Let the reader know the benefits of reading your book. Let the readers know what's in it for them.

## Building Your Media Kit

Your media kit (MK) should be both printed and online. Your MK is created to educate the press about you and your book.

It should look professional. Your MK is a great package to send to talk radio hosts, newspaper columnists, book reviewers, TV hosts or media people who have an audience that might be interested in your book. In today's market most journalists and TV hosts will prefer a link to your Web site.

Media people are busy. It is important that your media kit be clear and concise. If you have done a good job of telling them about you and your book in an engaging way, you will get the attention that you need to promote your book.

## The Message

Make sure that your message is clearly defined. Media professionals are looking for books that tie into the interests of their audiences. Be clear about the benefits of reading your book. If you can tie your subject to a news item, an issue of the day, a holiday or the anniversary of an historical event, it will help you get more coverage.  For example, if you are writing a book about feminism, time the book's release to coincide with women's suffrage month.

## Unique Features

Remember, your media kit will describe what is newsworthy or exciting about your book. The mere fact that you have published a book is not newsworthy. Tens of thousands of books are published each year. Figure out why your book is relevant to journalists and readers who you don't know. If your book is fiction, talk about the plot. Write about your book's timeliness and relevance to real-world issues. As an author, you are the expert. Think of yourself in those terms and don't be afraid to share your expertise.

## Media Kit Components

Pay attention to the "look and feel" of your kit. If you are doing an online kit and a hard copy kit, use the same typeface, graphics and color. Include a headshot, but make sure it is professionally done, but without looking staged.

Make sure the information in your kit is relevant and accurate. Contents may include:

- Two-pocket, glossy presentation folder
- One-page press release
- Author bio and photo
- Photocopies of reviews or links to online reviews
- Photocopies or scans of articles published by you or others about your book
- A review copy of your book or a postcard with an email link
- Promotional items such as bookmarks, T-shirts or coffee mugs
- Two business cards
- A one-page sample interview – a list of typical questions and answers
- A list of topics you are qualified to speak on
- A video or audio recording of a recent presentation, workshop, or radio/television or podcast interview.[11]
- A video book trailer (if you have the budget)[12]

## Radio and Television

Every day there are thousands of people who appear as guests on various TV and radio talk shows. You could be one of them! There is an old saying, "Grow where you're planted." When it comes to television and radio spots, this is certainly true. Always start in your own backyard. Don't worry about making a mistake; it is better to learn on a local 500-watt radio station, than fail spectacularly on a national talk show.

In many towns around the country, there are local radio and television talk shows and variety and specialty shows where you can talk about your

---

[11] The video should be three to five minutes long. The podcast can be slightly longer, but shouldn't exceed eight minutes.
[12] A book trailer is a short one to three minutes video advertising a book using multi-media visuals and sounds.

book. Target them carefully before contacting them. A great Web site and online media kit are critical.

### *Marketer's Note*

*Have a printer or Sam's Club print a stand-alone sign of the cover of your book. They can print a color copy on foam-core board, complete with fold-out cardboard legs for a free-standing sign. A free- standing sign that is 2' x 3' costs about $30. Use this when you make presentations, at book signings or book fairs. You can also have a smaller desktop version to put on your sales*
*table.*

The sample interview can be an invaluable tool for you as an author. Reporters and interviewers are busy people. They may not have time to read your entire book but would still like to interview you. Help them out by providing a list of questions and a summary of how you typically answer that question.

If your book covers a complex topic, then you may be able to speak on several different sub-topics that are covered in your book. If you have written multiple books, then you can talk about topics related to each book. Don't be shy about letting people know that you are well-versed on the topics covered in your book.

If you make it easy for a reporter or reviewer to interview you, then you can expect a better response from media people.

*Marketer's Note*

*To keep abreast of new developments in your field, set up a "Google Alert." Go to **http://google.com/alert** and enter the subject you want to search for. You can ask that articles be sent to you once a day or more often and you can set as many alerts as you like. If you don't have a Gmail account, you can send the alerts to another email address. I recommend setting up an independent email account just for alerts. They can come fast and clutter your regular mail account over time. Always set a Google alert for your name and the title of your book. Google alerts are a great way to pick up ideas for blog postings and ezine articles and track media coverage.*

Your press release should be written as soon as your book is written.

*Marketer's Note*

*If you want to know more about writing a press release buy The Associated Press Style Guidelines (available on Amazon). This book focuses on punctuation, use of abbreviations, spelling out numbers vs. use of numerals, and much more. Journalist and editors use AP style. By putting your press release in AP style, you automatically build credibility with the audience and appear more professional.*

## News Release 101

Consider the following when preparing your news release:

- Your topic should be compelling and of interest to a journalist.
- What is your purpose – what do you want to accomplish?
- Who is your audience and why will they be interested in this news?
- What media outlets are they most likely to read?
- What is the news "hook" or angle?
- Use Associated Press (AP) Style Guidelines for punctuation, abbreviation, capitalization, use of numbers, etc.
- Keep the headline to eight to ten, well-crafted, well-chosen words.
- *Don't* put the headline in all capitals.
- Use a verb in the headline to give it more energy and life.
- Use a sub-head to reinforce your newsworthy idea to the journalist reading your release.
- Dateline: city in all capitals and state (abbreviated using AP style), date (longer months abbreviated according to AP style). Contain the date in parentheses. Do not use ordinal numbers ($1^{st}$, $5^{th}$, etc.). The date is followed by an em dash with a space preceding and following it.
- In the body of your release, always put the most important news first (i.e., what is most important to the journalist or his or her audience, *not* what is most important to you).
- Plain English works best.
- Observe the journalists' rule: cover the basics (who, what, when, where, why, how).
- Use quotations only if they help make a valid point and contribute to the reader's understanding.
- Use a standard, easy-to-read font like Times New Roman. Use a 10- or 12-point type. Use double spacing or 1.5 spacing.

- Keep the release to one page if possible. If other information is critical, consider creating another page that is a fact sheet or backgrounder.
- Put author or publisher info at the bottom.
- At the end of the copy, put three number signs with a space between each.
- Be sure to include contact information: name of contact, phone number including area code, email address, and Web site. Contact info can go at the top or bottom of the release.
- Edit and proofread carefully and multiple times. Errors will diminish your credibility.

## Building your Media List

Building your media list should begin long before your book is written. If you don't have access to a list of reporters, radio hosts and interviewers, there are many resources you can use. The library is a great resource for building your list. Always start locally with a list of media from your town or city.

**www.bacons.com.** Get free lists of publication names, phone numbers and addresses. Lists are sorted by cities, general topic, and market.

**www.bookmarket.com/directories.** Get pages of data to help you assemble print media lists.

**www.gebbieinc.com.** You have to pay for this one. Gebbie offers a comprehensive directory. They don't have editors' names—you will have to get those yourself from each outlet's Web site. The lists are kept up to date.

**www.mediapost.com.** Get the publication names, addresses and phone numbers, but this source doesn't provide editor's names.

**www.dir.yahoo.com/news_and_media**

Carefully target the media. If you wrote a cookbook, don't send a press release to the mystery novel reviewer. Avoid the shotgun approach. It seldom works and can make journalist angry.

## Sample Press Release

### Self publishing goes mainstream

*New book helps authors sidestep traditional publishers to publish their own works*

LOUISVILLE, Ky., (May 1, 2011) — A revolution has begun in publishing. In 2009, 244,000 books were traditionally published, but more than 724,000 books were self published —181 percent more than in the previous year.

Traditional publishers, struggling with lower profits and increased competition, often favor well-known or celebrity authors whose books are likely to generate huge profits. First-time or unknown authors are often ignored. However, with the introduction of print-on-demand technology and the invention of the Espresso book machine (a revolutionary, high-speed digital press), it is now possible for modern authors to bypass traditional publishers and take their books directly to readers.

"Self publishing is no longer synonymous with self defeating," said Paul Nathan, in a column for *Publisher's Weekly*.

Peggy DeKay has just released a book that demystifies the process of self publishing. *Self Publishing for Virgins* guides first-time authors through the process of moving from raw manuscripts on their computers to perfect bound, self-published books — without spending thousands of dollars. DeKay's book shows authors how to get their titles on Amazon.com and in bookstores and libraries across the country. Her book teaches authors how to promote and market their books using social media and stealth marketing — a series of non-traditional techniques and approaches to book promotion. *Self Publishing for Virgins* is the definitive guide on how to self publish. It is available on Amazon and in retail bookstores.

DeKay is an award-winning writer and the editor of *POD WIRE*, an e-zine for authors interested in learning about self publishing. She is a former newspaper columnist and former editor of *Writer's Wire*. DeKay teaches self publishing workshops and frequently speaks at conferences. She lives in Louisville.

### #

**CONTACT:**
Your name here, imprint name here, [Web site address]
(111) 222-3333, email address
*Your Book Title,* your ISBN number here

## Certifications

Certifications are another way to quickly build your credibility. The National Speakers Association offers a professional certification (CSP-Certified Speaking Professional) for speakers who have given a certain number of paid speeches.

## Building Your Expert Status

You shouldn't rely solely on the fact that you are a published author to establish your credibility. Membership in carefully chosen organizations and associations can help to build credibility. If there are key associations in your area of expertise, then join the top one or two recognized groups. For example, if you are writing a book about how to build a speaking career, you should certainly belong to the National Speakers Association. Most writers should belong to at least one prestigious writing group; for example, the American Society of Journalists and Authors (ASJA) or the Author's Guild. To join the Author's Guild, you must be a published writer. The membership of $90 per year gives you access to other members who range from famous to not-so-famous authors, playwrights and screenwriters.

*The Society of Children's Book Writers and Illustrators* (SCBWI) is a great organization for writers of children's books. This organization has been around for more than 20 years and is one of the largest writers' organizations in the country. They also have regional chapters and each region has annual conferences that can be a great resource for children's book writers.

Society of Children's Book Writers & Illustrators
8271 Beverly Blvd.
Los Angeles, CA 90048
Phone: (323) 782-1010 (9 a.m. - 5:30 p.m. Pacific time)
Fax: (323) 782-1892
**scbwi@scbwi.org**
**www.scbwi.org**

Here are some other groups you may consider joining as you progress in your writing career.

The Authors Guild
31 East 32nd Street, 7th Floor
New York, NY 10016
Phone: (212) 563-5904
Fax: (212) 564-5363
**staff@authorsguild.org**
**www.authorsguild.org**

American Society of Journalists and Authors
1501 Broadway, Suite 403, New York, NY 10036
Phone: (212) 997-0947
Fax: (212) 937-2315
**www.asja.org**

Mystery Writers of America
1140 Broadway, Suite 1507
New York NY 10001
Phone: (212) 888-8171
Fax: (212) 888-8107
**www.mysterywriters.org**

Romance Writers of America
14615 Benfer Rd
Houston, TX 77069
Phone: (832) 717-5201
**www.rwa.org/cs/home**
info@rwa.org

## Writing Articles

Consider publishing excerpts of your book, or writing-related articles in
writers' magazines, trade magazines or e-zines. These outside
publication sources help establish you as an expert and can get your

book noticed. Let's say you have written a book about Himalayan cats. An article written in *Cat Fancy* magazine may attract the attention of tens of thousands of readers. Most magazine editors are willing to give you a by-line. Your by-line may include your name, Web site and/or email address. You can use the link to your CreateSpace landing page or Amazon Author Page.

The best time to send queries for a proposed article in a magazine is three to four months before the hoped-for publication date. Remember, most editors work on schedules far in advance.

 *Marketer's Note*

*Most magazines work on a 90- to 180-day turn-around time. If your book will be released in March, you need to approach magazine editors months before then. Many magazine editors work on seasonal articles and nearly everyone is working at least two months in advance of publication. E-zines or online magazines have a shorter lead time. Online publication can happen within days, especially if your topic is of interest and you have been published before.*

## Local Marketing

Never overlook the opportunities that exist in your own backyard. Does your city or town have a business journal or magazine? You should contact them first about writing an article about your topic if it is business related. Don't forget your local newspapers, newsletters and organizations. Consider alumni newsletters and Web sites. There are hundreds of ways, both traditional and non-traditional, to market your book. In the next chapter, we will talk about one of the most important markets for a self-published author— *Amazon.com.*

## Podcasting

A podcast is nothing more than a pre-recorded radio program that can be downloaded for free to an iPod or a compatible MP3 player. A podcast is a great way to generate interest in your book.

If you have never listened to a podcast, go to **www.itunes.com/podcasts**, pick one and listen. Starting your own podcast is not that hard and the startup costs can be less than $200.

### *Self Publisher's Checklist*

- ✓ *Write an outstanding author's bio.*
- ✓ *Put together your media kit using all the elements outlined.*
- ✓ *Assemble a carefully targeted media list and contact information.*

"*The profession of book-writing makes horse racing seem like a solid, stable business.* "

~John Steinbeck

# WHAT YOU WILL LEARN IN THIS CHAPTER

Author Central account

Maximizing Amazon online sales

Amazon Encore and Amazon Associate

Top reviewers, ranking, Listmania, tags

# 14 MAKE THE MOST OF AMAZON

*"Whenever you find yourself on the side of the majority, it's time to pause and reflect."*
~Mark Twain

In this chapter we will tackle the 600-pound gorilla in the room—Amazon.com. For a traditionally published and self-published author, Amazon cannot be ignored. If your book is to be successful, it should have a relatively high ranking on Amazon. Amazon ranks books for sale on its site *hourly*. To have a high-ranking book on Amazon isn't as hard as it might appear. With millions of titles for sale, the numbers look daunting. But never fear. Because of the algorithm that Amazon uses to rank books, an author who manages to sell 500 books in one day can go from a low ranking to a respectable one.

## Amazon Author Central

As a newly published author, you will want to establish your Amazon author's account. To learn about the features of an author's account on Amazon, use the link below:

**https://authorcentral.amazon.com/gp/help**

Entire books have been written about mining the benefits available to independent authors on Amazon. One of the best is *Aiming at Amazon,* by Aaron Shepherd. Shepherd has self published several books and has made maximizing online sales his specialty.

The good news is, if you are using CreateSpace to produce your book, then you are in a unique position to take advantage of the benefits of Amazon. Amazon is the parent company of CreateSpace and as such, the transition from selling on CreateSpace to selling on Amazon is seamless.

Once your book is published, you should set up and maintain your Amazon Author Central account.

Before you set up an author's account on Amazon, you should open a new Amazon account under your published name. Make a purchase with the new account to activate it. Once that's done, you are ready to set up your Author Central account. The Author Page on Amazon is where your readers can learn about you.

Here is some of the information available on Author Central:

- Author profile or biography
- Events
- Published books
- Blog
- Forums or communities
- Sales information
- Book trailers or photos (you can add up to eight videos and prioritize the order of their appearance on the page)

Changes to your Author Page will appear 24 hours after editing. As a CreateSpace publisher, your book listing on the Amazon sales page will automatically be listed. However, if you want to take advantage of the Amazon Author's Web site, you will need to set it up yourself.

To set up or edit your Author Page, go to:

**https://authorcentral.amazon.com/**

Your book should already be listed for sale on Amazon before you set up your author account.

 *Marketer's Note*

> *Book trailers can cost little or nothing to several thousand dollars. If you think you have the skills to do one; you can use Windows Movie Maker to edit your video or Roxio Pro software to edit slides and video.*

## Managing Your Author Profile

Information added to the Profile Tab of Author Central will be added automatically to your Author's Page.

To view a sample bio, go to:
**www.amazon.com/-/e/B000AQ0UA4**

To edit your profile, visit the Profile page at:
**www.amazon.com/gp/pdp/profile/**

If you have purchased items on Amazon and have a user account, Amazon will likely recognize you when you log in using the edit Profile link. If you are working on your Author Page, always log in with the account that matches your publication name.

## Changing View Settings

You can decide which elements of your profile can be seen by visitors. To change or set viewing permission, go to your Profile Page using the profile link above, then click "Edit Your Profile" button on the top right corner of the page. Choose the setting you want:
Private (only you can see it)
Friends (only Amazon Friends will see the information)
Everyone (everyone will see your latest activity on your Profile page)

## Adding Friends on Amazon

If you want to add someone as a "friend" on Amazon, go to his or her profile and click "*Add to interesting people,*" then check, "*also mark as Amazon friend.*"

## Favorite Items Section

The Favorite Items section of the Profile lets you share your favorite books, music or other items with Amazon.com visitors.

## Sales Information

Amazon has some wonderful sales information available to you as an Amazon author. You can not only see how many books you have sold, but where they were sold. This can be very useful information and can, over time, tell you where to concentrate your marketing efforts.

As a CreateSpace author, or a Kindle author you will have access to sales data of your book through the Reports feature in CreateSpace. Your sales may not be reflected under the Sales Info Tab of your Author Central account.

If your book qualifies for the Bookstores & Online Retailers outlet of the expanded Distribution Channel through CreateSpace, you will be able to see your sales figures in Author Central, Sales Info tab.

## Sales Info Tab

The Sales Info tab in Author Central helps you identify sales trends. If you have more than one book in your bibliography, the Sales Info tab defaults to an All Books view, which displays your total books sold, combined.

To see a specific title, click the orange triangle next to the All Books heading and select the title. To see data for a specific format of a book, scroll down to Sales by Week from BookScan. The bar chart shows copies sold of each format the book is printed in.

## Geographic Sales

BookScan divides the continental U.S. into geographic areas, known as Designated Market Areas (DMAs). DMAs are organized by zip codes, and are typically named after the largest city within the area.

## Amazon Ranking

If you are viewing a specific title, the Amazon Bestsellers Rank History section shows a chart of your title's ranking over time. Rankings are updated every hour, 24 hours a day. In the "All Books view," the Bestsellers Rank shows the ranking summary of the top three ranked books. Bestsellers Rank ranks *all* books, one against the other. The lower the ranking number, the higher the ranking and the more books that have been sold. A book with a rank of #1 is the best-selling book.

The chart compares your book with all other books for sale, so individual sales of your book might not result in a change in ranking. For example:

- **A copy of your book sold, but the Bestsellers Rank did not change.** Your book may have been purchased recently, but if books in the rest of the catalog have recently been purchased more often than yours, your rank may remain constant or might drop.

- **The Bestsellers Rank changed by 25,000, but you hadn't sold any books.** Your book's rank can and will change even though its sales may not have changed. If you are selling one or two books a week, and the other books have not sold more copies, your ranking can move up over time.

- **When your ranking fluctuates and other books in your genre don't.** Bestsellers Rank is calculated over the entire sales history. That means that if your book has sold consistently over time, it's ranking will remain steady. It's a numbers game. Selling one copy of a book with a low overall number can make the ranking fluctuate, while selling one copy of a book with consistent sales over time most likely will not change the ranking.

The good news is that if your book is new, or has had relatively low rankings historically, you can change the ranking from dismal to respectable in a day if you can sell several hundred copies.

Since Amazon ranks books hourly, if you expect your rankings to increase because of an event, or an appearance on a television show or on a talk radio show, take a screen shot of your ranking. This will allow you to say that you are a "top-ranked Amazon author" and prove it!

## Tags

Tagging is a way for more people to find your book. Let's say you have written a book about mountain climbing in the Andes, and your book specifically targets preparation and equipment. Someone may buy your book and set up a tag for *mountain climbing*, while another reader may say *mountain climbing equipment*, and a third may tag your book under *Andes*.

Tags don't just help customers find your book; they also help Amazon categorize books. This is good for you, because it will help your book move into new groupings that may be seen by customers who know nothing about your book.

As a new author, you should set up some tags for your own book right away. Each reader can place up to 15 tags. To get started, place at least 10 to 12 tags for your book. Your tags will show up at the bottom of your book listing (scroll down to the bottom of the page), with a green check. Tags that are listed but not checked have been placed on your book listing page by other people.

Will just a few tags make a difference? Perhaps not, but 100 tags placed by 100 different people will move your book up in the searches, exposing your book to more buyers.

To increase rankings, you can add the following information to your book's product detail page:

**Cover art**—This is done automatically if you are using CreateSpace.

**Search Inside**—This allows customers to read excerpts from your book online. This feature is automatically set up by CreateSpace.

**Description**—This is no longer automatically set up by CreateSpace.

**Review Excerpts**—Readers like to know what others are saying about your book. Including excerpts from reviews is a good way to promote your book.

## Amazon Editorial Review

Amazon's editorial team does review some books. If you want to send a copy of your book for possible review or a feature, send it via the U.S. Postal Service. Before you do, you will need to review Amazon's extensive list of subject areas to get the right category for your book. Getting the category correctly identified will expedite the request for a review.

Send your book and a cover letter to:

**Amazon.com**
Attn. Editorial – [Product & Category]
701 Fifth Avenue
Suite 1500
Seattle WA 98104

## Amazon Customer Reviews

Getting customer reviews for your book is important. Ask your friends or family members, or other readers to write a review. Ideally they will write a positive review. Many Amazon shoppers rely on reviews to help them make their buying decisions, so getting your customers to review your book is important.

Never ask anyone to review your book who hasn't read it. This will ultimately make you look amateurish and a phony review can be spotted a mile away. If we, as a book-buying community want to continue to rely on reviews as a gauge to purchasing, then the reviews posted should be from people who have read the book they are reviewing.

Six positive reviews are ideal. Once your book is listed for sale on Amazon, you will have a link to your sales page. When someone contacts you about your book and compliments you, thank them, and send a link to your book and ask them to write a review.

Not all reviews are positive. If you get a negative review, it isn't the end of the world. Most authors who have sold lots of books have received a few bad reviews. As Donald Trump is credited with saying, "Bad press is better than no press at all."

## Top Reviewers

There are a special group of people who review books on a regular basis on Amazon. They are called Top Reviewers. Harriet Klausner has reviewed over 24,000 books! Top Reviewers help people make good buying decisions every day on Amazon. You can tell if a review is done by a Top Reviewer by the "Top Reviewer Badge" that will be placed beside the review.

Getting a positive review for your book from a Top Reviewer can help sell more books. Top Reviewers are busy and asking them for a review should be taken seriously and done professionally. Never ask a Top Reviewer to give you a positive review.

*If you want a positive review, write a great book!*

Here is a list of the top ten reviewers:

1. Harriet Klausner
2. Lawrance M. Bernabo
3. E. A. Solinas
4. Grady Harp
5. Gail Cooke
6. Rebecca Johnson
7. Professor Donald Mitchell
8. Joanna Daneman
9. W. Boudville
10. Fr. Kurt Messick

**www.amazon.com/review**

Recently Amazon has changed the way they rank Top Reviewers. One of the principle criteria for a Top Reviewer now is "review helpfulness." Amazon determines how helpful reviews are by what customers reading the review have to say.

Study the Top Reviewers list. Pick reviewers who review a lot of books in your genre. When asking for a review, send a brief email asking if you can send them a review copy of your book. If they agree, send the book with a short, concise cover letter thanking them for the review. Let them know that the review copy is theirs to keep. Send out 50 to 75 books to get 15 or 20 reviews.

## Listmania

Lists on Amazon are just that—book lists that the reader compiles and shares with other readers. It could be a list of your favorite cookbooks, mysteries, or a list of how-to books. As an author, you should create lists of your favorite books and *always put your book on the list.*

For example, if your book is released in 2011, then create a list of *My Favorite New Books in 2011*. One of your favorite new books will be your own.

### Create a Listmania List

Go to your profile page at **www.amazon.com/gp/pdp/profile/** and log in. Click EDIT YOUR PROFILE on the top right, then click the LISTS tab in the Contributions section.

1. Click CREATE YOUR FIRST ONE NOW or if you already have lists, click MANAGE YOUR LISTMANIA LIST.
2. Compile your list and hit the PREVIEW button. If you like what you see, hit PUBLISH LIST.
3. Add tags to your list. This will allow you to add keywords. The keywords will help people discover your list, and your book.

### Amazon Associate

Launched in 1996, Associates is Amazon's affiliate marketing program. By linking to Amazon products and services, you can add compelling content for your site visitor's enjoyment and receive 4 to 8 percent in referral fees for doing so. If an visitor comes to Amazon's site from your link, you can receive a referral fee on anything they purchase in that 24-hour period. To learn more: **https://affiliate-program.amazon.com.**

## Amazon Encore

Amazon Encore (AE) is an imprint of Amazon. Amazon Encore is modeled after the traditional publisher model except that AE focuses on self-published authors who have self published with CreateSpace.

Because it is so new, no one knows how effective it will be. The Encore program will use information such as customer reviews appearing on Amazon.com to identify "exceptional, overlooked books and authors with more potential than their sales may indicate." Amazon will then work with these authors to help re-introduce their books to potential readers through marketing efforts and by using expanded distribution channels like Kindle books, audible.com and the Amazon Book Store. Amazon will also leverage its network of national and independent bookstores. Books are chosen by Amazon. You cannot sign up for Amazon Encore.

### *Marketer's Note*

*The launch of Amazon Encore means that it is even more important to garner customer reviews and take full advantage of your Amazon Author's Account.*

### *Self Publisher's Checklist*

- ✓ *Set up your Author Central account.*
- ✓ *Compile a list of 50 to 75 top reviewers for your genre.*
- ✓ *Send them an email, letter and review copy of your book asking for a review.*
- ✓ *Set up your Author Central pages.*
- ✓ *Create a list in Listmania and include your book in the list.*

- ✓ *Write and add at least 10 tags for your book.*
- ✓ *Ask your favorite readers to post a review of your book on Amazon and send a copy of your book to the Amazon Editorial Review.*
- ✓ *Sign up to become an Amazon Associate.*

# WHAT YOU WILL LEARN IN THIS CHAPTER

How libraries
buy books

Marketing to
libraries

Quality Books,
Inc.

working with a
distributor

CreateSpace
Expanded
Channel and
Baker & Taylor

# 15 MARKET TO LIBRARIES

*"Life is either a daring adventure, or nothing."*          *~Helen Keller*

In this chapter, you will learn how to market your book to libraries. If you are writing non-fiction, the library market can be quite lucrative. In the U.S. there are approximately 20,000 library branches. Most branches carry their own acquisitions budget.

While you can and should approach the library branches in your town or city, contacting each library in the U.S. would be too costly. There is a better way—Baker & Taylor and Quality Books.

## Distributors

For book distribution to the U.S. library market, Baker & Taylor and Quality Books are specialists. Both employ sales representatives who call on library markets throughout the U.S. That means if your book is accepted, they will use their sales force to represent your book, along with many others, to libraries all over the country.

Quality Books has a significant sales force that regularly call on libraries in the U.S. Take advantage of their clout by letting them represent your book. This is where your book's sale price becomes important. Wholesale distributors make money by buying your books at a 45-55 percent discount and then reselling those books to libraries. Because wholesale distributors generally work off gross profits after the sale of your book to an end user (in this case, the library), the realistic percentage winds up being higher. This is why you need to price your book at a minimum of five to eight times your delivered price. As you can see, the price of your book is critical to realizing profits after discounts.

## CIP and Quality Books

As noted in an earlier chapter, a CIP (Catalog in Publication) is a catalog listing that is printed on the copyright page of your book. To qualify for a CIP listing, you have to have published at least three books. Why have a CIP? If you are a small publisher, a CIP makes you look bigger. Many publishers get around the three-book rule by opting to have Quality Books carry their books.

If you would like to have Quality Books represent your book, call and ask for their NEW Book Information form and a sample of their Distribution to Libraries Agreement. Their Web site is **http://quality-books.com.**

## What Libraries Buy

Libraries want books that will be a resource for their readers. Librarians will look for books that have been reviewed in *Library Journal, Literary Marketplace, Publisher's Weekly* or *Kirkus Reviews*.

Most libraries won't acquire books that have fill-in-the-blank pages because they don't want patrons to mark in the books. Comb-bound books (books with a large wire or plastic spiral binding that holds the pages together) don't hold up over time and are also unpopular. Your book should be a standard trim size and have a readable spine to sell best to the library.

If you have written a non-fiction book that you hope to sell to libraries, it should have an index, a bibliography and other resource pages. Remember, libraries want good resource books for their readers. Good resource books have lots of back matter.

If you want to market your book to libraries (and this can be a very lucrative market), here is what you will need:

1. LCCN
2. ISBN
3. Barcode
4. Copyright
5. PCIP or CIP (optional)
6. Index or glossary
7. Resource page/s
8. Bibliography
9. Table of contents

If your book is fiction, you will not need all 10 items.

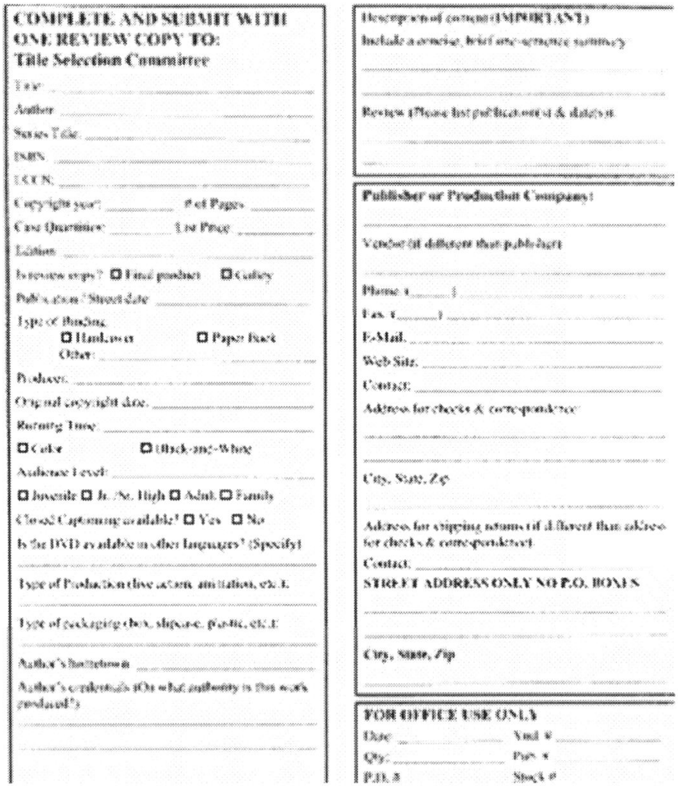

COMPLETE AND SUBMIT WITH ONE REVIEW COPY TO:
**Title Selection Committee**

Title
Author
Series Title
ISBN
LCCN
Copyright year · # of Pages
Case Quantities · List Price
Edition
Is review copy? ☐ Final product ☐ Galley
Publication / Street date
Type of Binding: ☐ Hardcover ☐ Paper Back Other
Producer
Original copyright date
Running Time
☐ Color ☐ Black-and-White
Audience Level: ☐ Juvenile ☐ Jr./Sr. High ☐ Adult ☐ Family
Closed Captioning available? ☐ Yes ☐ No
Is the DVD available in other languages? (Specify)
Type of Production (live action, animation, etc.)
Type of packaging (box, slipcase, plastic, etc.)
Author's hometown
Author's credentials (On what authority is this work produced?)

Description of content (IMPORTANT)
Include a concise, brief one-sentence summary
Reviews (Please list publication(s) & date(s))

**Publisher or Production Company:**
Vendor (if different than publisher)
Phone
Fax
E-Mail
Web Site
Contact
Address for checks & correspondence
City, State, Zip
Address for shipping returns (if different than address for checks & correspondence)
Contact
STREET ADDRESS ONLY NO P.O. BOXES
City, State, Zip

**FOR OFFICE USE ONLY**
Date · Vnd #
Qty · Pub #
P.O. # · Stock #

**Figure 15.1** New Book Form

Library budgets are for a fiscal year. They tend to purchase at the beginning of the year through June. By the end of the year, the budget is usually depleted and acquisitions will slow down. If you are marketing your book to libraries through Quality Books and Baker & Taylor and your book is popular, you can sell between 100-600 copies or more in a year. Since library books wear out over time, you may have repeat orders for the following year or years.

Why is the library market so desirable? Libraries spend in excess of $1.5 billion each year for books. About 3,000 libraries have a budget of

$25,000 or more.  Because they don't have unlimited budgets, they have to be selective about the books they buy.

## Changing Market

More and more libraries are turning to audio and e-books. Right now Adobe Systems is working on a new standard for e-books that will be available to libraries in the U.S. It is called the ePUB Standard. As this standard progresses and becomes widely accepted, e-books will become more and more prominent in the industry. If you have published a perfect bound book, you should also be thinking seriously about producing your book in electronic and audio formats.

## Library Reviews

Most librarians rely on reviews to choose books. Librarians read *Library Journal, Kirkus Reviews, Choice* and *Publisher's Weekly.* To get a review from one of these publications, you will need to send a copy of your book, along with a letter about the book. If your book has been reviewed by your local newspaper or you have great blurbs from well-known people on your back cover, mention them in your letter. Be sure to include a one-page data sheet on your book. The data sheet should have: LCCN or CPIP, copyright year, ISBN, title, sub-title, author's name, publisher's data and retail price. It should also give a synopsis of your book. Listed below are the addresses and phone numbers for reviewers:

*Choice* magazine is a resource for academic libraries. They publish nearly 7,000 reviews annually. *Choice* reviews roughly 25 to 30 percent of the titles submitted. Choice magazine reviews scholarly works.

**www.ala.org/ala/mgrps/divs/acrl/publications/choice/infoforpub/infor mationpublishers.cfm**

*Kirkus Reviews*—See guidelines at **http://kirkusreviews.com.**

*Library Journal*—Books are selected for their potential interest to a broad spectrum of libraries. They prefer to receive materials three to four months in advance of publication date.

**www.libraryjournal.com/csp/cms/sites/LJ/SubmitToLJ/TitlesForReview.csp**

**Publisher's Weekly** is the premier weekly magazine for publishers. **www.publishersweekly.com/pw/corp/submissionguidelines.html**

Unique Books operates similarly to Quality Books. They have sales representatives who work for them and make presentations to libraries around the country. They also exhibit at library conferences. If you wish to contact specific libraries that you feel will want to carry your book, you can obtain lists of libraries from these resources:

**www.sla.org**
**http://galegroup.com**
**http://lists.webjunction.org/libweb**
**http://Publiclibraries.com**

## Expanded Distribution

The Expanded Distribution option in CreateSpace is a great thing for the self-published author. According to a CreateSpace sales representative, the Expanded Channel program sets up a distribution arrangement for your book with Ingram Books and Baker & Taylor.

Ingram Books, as you may recall from earlier chapters, is the largest book distributor in the U.S. Does this mean that your book will be sold on other Amazon sites like www.Amazon.UK? Not necessarily, according to a CreateSpace representative. "That depends on the individual book, and the attention that it gets in the marketplace."

Baker & Taylor is also a huge distributor and one of the main book distributors in the U.S. Baker & Taylor also markets to U.S. libraries. Having a distribution arrangement with both can only help you as a self-published author.

CreateSpace won't divulge what their arrangements are with Ingram Books and Baker & Taylor. What they will tell you is that you will make a 40 percent royalty or commission on each book sold through the Expanded Distribution Channel. Here's an example:

| | |
|---|---|
| Retail book price | $15.00 |
| Print cost | ($2.15) |
| Expanded Channel Commission | ($5.41) |
| *(40 percent of the list price per book sold)* | |
| **Your Royalty** | **$7.44** |

### *Marketer's Note*

*If you want to sell your books to libraries, I encourage you to apply to Quality Books to see if they will represent and distribute your book. This only applies to the author who has decided to form a publishing company. If you want to know more, the American Library Association (www.ala.org) has an excellent resource called Marketing to Library Associations.*

### *Self Publisher's Checklist*

✓ *Sign up for the Pro Plan through Create Space.*
✓ *Contact Quality Books (if you are a publisher) and complete their Book Information Form.*

# WHAT YOU WILL LEARN IN THIS CHAPTER

Web designers vs.
DIY

Author Web sites

Fee and free Web
sites:

Blogger, Weebly,
WordPress and
BlueHost

List building and
e-stores

# 16 CREATE AN AUTHOR WEB SITE

*"Having heard all of this, you may choose to look the other way…but you can never say again that you did not know."*

~William Wilberforce

In this chapter, you will learn what is important to have on your author's Web site and how to create the best one you can on a budget. We will talk about what type of software to use to build your site and how to pick a good Web site hosting service. We will also talk about list building, e-store, resources for readers and how to build your author platform by taking advantage of your Web presence.

## Web Site Basics

Let's talk about Web sites. Authors sell only one product—words! I bet you thought I was going to say "books" didn't you? When it comes to creating a Web site, don't think of yourself as an author, but as a business person who is in the business of selling words. Your words may often be in the form of books, but they may also be speeches, presentations, tutorials, special reports or e-books!

An effective author site in today's online environment cannot be a static advertisement for your book. Author sites should be dynamic, informational and conversational. What do I mean? Your author site should be a destination, not an advertisement. It should offer your reader further discussion about your topic.

As an author, you are in a unique position. One of the most profitable things sold on the Internet today is information—words. As a writer, words are your stock and trade. Use your skill as a writer to write an intriguing author bio, a super blog and even generate some special reports. Let's take a hypothetical case. Writing for the Internet is different than book writing. To be successful, use brevity, combined with a high level of content.

**Case Study:** Jane Doe is a cat breeder. She breeds Himalayan cats and sells them to other breeders and to individuals. She has been doing this for 20 years and is considered an expert in cat breeding. In 2010, she self published a book about Himalayan cats called *All About Himalayan Cats*.

What should she do first? Jane should buy her domain names. Domain names can be purchased from sites like godaddy.com for about $10 each. The domain name in this case is janedoe.com. She should purchase two domain names, one is *Jane Doe.com* and the second is *allabouthimalayancats.com* and perhaps a third domain name might be *aahc.com*.

Now that she has her domain names reserved, it is time to make some decisions about her Web site. There are three basic choices: pay to have a web designer create your site, use a free site, or use a service provider that has templates you can customize.

## Hiring a Web Designer

If you hire a designer to create your site, expect to pay from $250 to over $1,200, depending on the complexity of the site. Some Web designers charge $2,500 or more! To find a developer if you are on a budget, try **http://elance.com**. Elance is a freelance hiring site. You bid your job out, then choose the designer and the price you like best from competing bids.

If you are thinking of using a designer, there is something else you need to consider. What happens if you want to change or update content on your site? What if you want to add a new book you've published, add a blog, or create a special report for your readers? You will have to call your designer, communicate your changes, and then wait for the designer to get it done. You will also have to pay for each change. What if your Web master or designer moves or quits?

## Free Sites

If you have minimal technical skills and a stout heart, you can dive in and create an author's site using free tools that are available on the Web. The downside to using free sites is site security—sometimes free sites can be deleted and the URLs (web addresses) for free sites can be long and cumbersome, not a small consideration if you are using your Web site to promote your book and other writing-related activities.

Here are the main players when it comes to free sites:

### www.Blogger.com

Blogger is easy to use and one of the more popular free sites. Blogger is a part of the Google family of products. If you are thinking of using Blogger.com, there are several good books available that can walk you through the process.

**www.Wordpress.org**

There are two WordPress sites. **Http://wordpress.org** is a free blogging platform, but will require that you sign up with a host or ISP (Internet Service Provider). When using WordPress, it is always better to use a host that has a control panel, called c-panel. The c-panel will ensure that your WordPress template can be loaded quickly and easily. I like Bluehost.com for WordPress, but GoDaddy.com also works well.

The second WordPress site is: **www.WordPress.com**

This is a free site and won't require an ISP or host. If you are opting for a free site to start with, I think taking the time to learn WordPress will benefit you down the road if and when you decide to get a hosted site. Once you set up your blog, the address or URL will look like this: **www.yourname.wordpress.com.**

## Google Pages

If you like Google and you use Gmail for your email account, you can use Google Pages. Google Pages has templates that can make building your site easier. The templates help you get a site up in hours instead of days or weeks. To see a tutorial on how to use Google Pages, use this link:

**www.google.com/sites/help/intl/en/overview.html**

To create your Web site using Google Pages, go to **www.sites.google.com**.

*Marketer's Note*

*Be careful about using free sites. Backups should be made frequently as free sites have been known to lose data from time to time. Since you are not paying for the service to begin with, there is little or no recourse if your site's data is lost. Backing up your online data is always a good idea.*

**www.weebly.com**

Weebly.com is a free site. It was one of *Time Magazine's* "50 Best Web sites of the Year." It's easy to use and you can set up e-commerce (a script or short program that allows people to purchase books on your site),and upload photos and videos. Again, it is a free site, and, as such, you need to be mindful of the possibility of lost data.

## Fee-Based Sites

*Hosted sites with templates*

**GoDaddy.com** has a wonderful site with lots of templates. A friend of mine literally built her site overnight using a GoDaddy template. GoDaddy is inexpensive, reliable and has the bells and whistles you need to create an author's site.

If you are planning to use WordPress as your Web site and blogging platform (which I recommend), **http://BlueHost.com** is a good hosting site. Bluehost has a control panel (c-panel) that gives you a dashboard-style central control panel for your site. It also will install WordPress with one-click efficiency. If you don't want to use WordPress, then GoDaddy.com or webbly.com are both good sites to use.

GoDaddy.com, like weebly.com, has pre-designed templates that, with a little bit of study, can be adapted to any author's requirements. The templates do most of the work for you. You can personalize any template with graphics and individualized navigation bars.

Once our cat book author has her Web site ready, she should set up her social media accounts—LinkedIn, Twitter and Facebook. These should be linked to her Web site. Because our author plans to speak to animal rights groups and cat breeder associations across the country, she will want to let people know on her Web site that she's available for speaking engagements.

WordPress has thousands of templates to choose from.  Many of them are free, but some templates are fee-based. My favorite is Thesis. Thesis costs a one-time fee of $79. For an additional $110 you can upgrade to a developer's package. This will allow you to use the Thesis template on multiple sites.

There are many WordPress designers who will build your Web site using a WordPress template for around $800. It's easy, once you are familiar with the process, to build a complex site using a WordPress template. There will be a learning curve, but once you have mastered it, you can modify your site at will—without paying a designer.

There are several great books on WordPress, both the free and the hosted version.  One that I like is *Sams Teach Yourself Word Press in 10 Minutes* by Chuck Tomasi and Kreg Steppe. There is also a great tutorial on Thesis at www.PodCastAnswerMan.com. (A $39 fee applies.)

## List Building

As an author, one of the main things you will want to do is build your platform. This can be done by collecting emails from seminars, book signings and other hands-on promotions, but your best and easiest way to build a list is to offer some good content on your site. Many authors give away e-books, or several chapters of their latest book in exchange for getting the Web site visitor's name and email address.

If you have written a non-fiction, how-to book, you may want to give away a free report on the topic of your book. Make it worthwhile, something that the average reader of your book couldn't easily get from another source. If your book is a memoir, or you write romance novels, you might want to give away several chapters of your latest book in advance in exchange for your visitor's information.

Don't be shy about giving away valuable information. It will always come back to you multi-fold! There's a great story told by Seth Godin, the bestselling author of *The Purple Cow*. After releasing a bestselling book, he read a book called *Tipping Point Two*, and was so inspired that he wrote a book called *Unleashing the Idea Virus* in 24 hours. He sent an email to his publishers telling them that he had his next book, and that he wanted to give away copies of it for free on the Internet. The publisher sent him back an email saying they couldn't give the book away, and that it would take 18 months to get his new book to market. Frustrated, he put his money where his mouth was, and posted the book his Web site and gave it away for free! In several months, people had downloaded millions of copies. Since he gave it away for free, he hadn't made any money. Then a funny thing happened—people started emailing him, asking for the free downloaded book in print form. Responding to the demand, he self published the book and sold it on Amazon for $40 each! It was a runaway hit. Godin made millions. The moral: sometimes giving something away is the best possible form of advertising. *Don't be afraid to be a resource for your readers!*

## E-store

An e-store, sometimes called e-commerce, is a program written for the express purpose of allowing customers to purchase goods and services online, from a Web site. This program, once installed on your Web site, gives you the ability to accept PayPal and credit cards. Some sites charge for this program, but most of the time you can load free e-store software and sell books on your site in a matter of hours. Keep in mind, transaction fees do apply.

## Sell through Amazon or DIY?

Once you have set up an e-store on your site, you will have the option to refer sales to yourself, or to Amazon. Why would I want to sell my own books from my own Web site through Amazon, you ask? Here's why.

As a published author, you can greatly benefit by becoming a high-ranking author on Amazon. Becoming an Amazon Bestselling Author will give you more clout, publicity and potential for ongoing book sales than nearly any type of marketing that you do on your own.

Amazon is the 600-pound gorilla in the room, and as such should be kept well-fed and happy! As a self-published author, Amazon and indie bookstores are your best friends. Besides, do you really want to spend your time shipping books, one at a time, to customers all over the country? Spend your time writing, and sell your books at speaking events.

**Marketer's Note**

*I knew an author who had published her book with a very small press. So small in fact, that she was their only client. They did have an agreement with distributors and if they sold the book online with Amazon , the author would have made only pennies on each sale. She declined to sell the book on Amazon, citing low commissions. Let's think about that decision for a minute. Could selling her book on Amazon have given her more credibility? Would it have exposed her book to millions of potential readers? Could she have created an Author Central page and driven more visitors to her Web site? The answers to these questions are YES! My recommendation is to always have your book for sale on Amazon. Luckily, as a Create Space author, your book is guaranteed to be for sale on Amazon.*

## Resources

Let's talk about your resource tab on your Web site. What can you offer your readers? What value can you add? It depends on the type of book you have written and on what types of books you may write in the future.

If you are primarily a non-fiction writer, you might want to offer your readers special reports. In the case of the woman who wrote about cats, "*The Top Ten Ways to Keep your Himalayan Cat Healthy and Fit*" might be a great report to give away to her Web site visitors.

- Make sure that the report is something your readers want and need.
- Make sure it's something that they couldn't have easily gotten another way.
- Make sure it's something with a high perceived value.

## Adding Videos

Adding videos to the welcome page of your site can give your Web site more excitement, a higher perceived value, and it keeps your visitors on your welcome page longer. This is a good thing. Statistically, the longer a visitor stays on your page, the more likely they are to buy. If you are thinking about videos, you can open a YouTube account. It is free and you can create your own videos. Keep them short—under three minutes.

Go to YouTube.com and select "create an account." Fill out the information they ask for and get to work.

## Web Site Sales Techniques

Let's use our case study. Our Himalayan cat author has collected the names of reputable breeders all over the country. She has also created many written procedures and hints about how to make the most of raising Himalayans. All of this material, while useful, is not fully covered in her book. She has created several special reports about raising and breeding Himalayans, as well. What can she do with this information? She can compile the information into one or several special reports. Save it to a PDF file and sell it on her Web site. Many authors, such as Dan Miller of 48days.com, have been packaging and selling "binder books" from their Web sites for many years. Because this information is not available anywhere except on the author's Web site, the perceived value is greater. It is not uncommon for authors to sell these special reports for $49 or more.

## Summary

Let's get back to our case study: the Himalayan cat author's site. Whether she chooses Blogger, WordPress, Google Pages, Weebly.com or a hosted site, our cat breeder will want to sell products, write a blog, or send out a newsletter. She will also want to capture the email addresses of visitors who come to her Web site.

Here are some suggestions for your Web site:

- Add an embedded video that tells people about your book.

- Provide resource pages that are free and can be downloaded. This builds content on your site and makes visitors want to come back for more.
- A blog is a must-have for writers. Blogs can bring additional traffic to your site, and can raise awareness of you and your book.
- Consider a free offer that can be downloaded in exchange for the visitor's email address.
- Include an author's statement. Check out Janet Evanovich's site at **http:/janetevanovich.com.** Read her author's bio and you can appreciate her use of humor.
- Include a "contact us" button, a "sign up" button, and a "buy now" button with a link to Amazon.
- Include a newsletter and a newsletter sign-up button on your site.

### *Self Publisher's Checklist*

- ✓ *Choose an Internet provider for your Web site.*
- ✓ *Sign up for one year.*
- ✓ *Link this site to your Amazon.com landing page.*
- ✓ *Post a book excerpt on your Web site.*
- ✓ *Put a sign-up box on your Welcome page.*
- ✓ *Put a "buy now" button on your site.*
- ✓ *Create tabs for "About the Author," "Contact Us," "Resources," "Bookstore" and "Blog."*

# WHAT YOU WILL LEARN IN THIS CHAPTER

Facebook fan pages,
Twitter, LinkedIn

Using social media

Specialty sites for
authors

Filedby
and
Goodreads

# 17 USING SOCIAL MEDIA

*"The best time to plan a book is while you are doing the dishes."*
*~Agatha Christie*

## Why Use Social Media

Why social media? Here are some amazing statistics on Facebook, the anchor site of social media today:

- There are more than 500 million active users.

- Fifty percent of active users log on to Facebook in any given day.

- An average user has 130 friends.

- People spend over 700 billion minutes per month on Facebook.

## Activity on Facebook

- There are over 900 million objects that people interact with (pages, groups, events and community pages).

- The average user is connected to 80 community pages, groups and events.[i]

- The average user creates 90 pieces of content each month.

- More than 30 billion pieces of content (Web links, news stories, blog posts, notes, photo albums, etc.) are shared each month.

## Global Reach

- More than 70 translations are available on the site.
- About 70 percent of Facebook users are outside of the United States.
- Over 300,000 users helped translate the site.

## Facebook

The Facebook motto is "Giving people the power to share and make the world more open and connected." Both Bing and Google now include Facebook and Twitter posts in their searches. This means that being on Facebook and Twitter can lead people to your Web site.

Facebook has not only changed the way individuals communicate with each other, it has changed the way countries communicate with each other. Many authors complain that being on Facebook takes time away from doing what they do best—*writing.* I can't say that I disagree. But Facebook, like exercise, must be done at least 20 minutes per day, three days per week, or you risk becoming flabby and out of shape!

Take a look at Janet Evanovich's Facebook page promoting her new comic series "Troublemaker." Here's the link:

**www.facebook.com/TroublemakerComics**

On her Facebook page, you can read excerpts of her forthcoming books or request a bookplate. These are clever and easy ways to get your readers engaged.

## Facebook Fan Page

A Facebook fan page looks exactly like a regular Facebook page with one major difference. On a regular page, you are limited to 5,000 friends. After that, Facebook will cut you off—just like that—no apologies. Your Facebook page will be gone and you will have to start all over.

A fan page is more like a business page. You can have as many fans as you want and you can build your fan base over time.

The other great advantage to a fan page is that after you have 125 fans, you can obtain a shorter URL. Before we go any further, know these four things about promoting your book or yourself on Facebook.

## Four Keys to a Successful Fan Page

1. Keep your information current.
2. Be relevant; don't post meaningless stuff.
3. Photos attract attention and promote interaction.
4. Stay interactive by responding to posts promptly.

If your book is published, you should have a Facebook fan page with the same title as your book. Once you know the name of your book, set up a fan page right away. You can keep it offline until your book is ready to be published. Since Facebook has a photo gallery, use it to post an image of your cover art. You can even ask people to vote on their favorite cover if you are trying to decide betweem several options. You can also post events and images on your fan page.

## aWeber

Facebook pages are getting more sophisticated and diverse every day. aWeber is a site that allows you to enhance the look and functionality of your Facebook fan page without having to know FBML (Facebook Markup Language) coding language. aWeber is a fee-based site and currently charges $19 per month for basic services. To see what an aWeber enhanced site can do for your Facebook fan page, see **www.facebook.com/socialnetworkingacademy.**

You can also use aWeber to build lists on Facebook, send out newsletters, schedule email campaigns and much more. aWeber is an auto responder. That means that you can schedule a series of mailings to a particular list and then tell the auto responder when you want those messages sent and to which list. To find out more about aWeber, go to **https://www.aweber.com/landing.htm.**

## Twitter

Twitter calls itself a "real-time, short messaging service that works over multiple networks and devices." Twitter is huge and growing very fast. Surprisingly, it has become the traditional publisher's tool of choice for social media. In early 2010, there were more than 75 million users broadcasting 50 million tweets per day.

Because of the finite length of a tweet or message sent over Twitter (140 characters), this medium lends itself more to a no-nonsense message. Remember, much like Facebook, blatant promotion is usually not the best way to proceed. Because users can search by subject matter or by URL, then it is likely that you may pick up some followers and bring them to your Web site.

Create a custom page and use your photo or another image to make your page more user-friendly. Next you will want to find the leaders of whatever niche you are targeting. If your book is on Himalayan cats, then search for leaders who talk about Himalayan cats. If they have lots of followers, then read their tweets and begin to follow their followers. To manage your Tweets, use **Hootsuite.com** or **Tweetdeck.com**. These will allow you to schedule tweets for days or weeks in advance.

## Tiny URLs

If you create an account with bit.ly or TinyURL.com you can post shortened versions of your links. This is especially useful with Twitter because you are so limited in the number of characters you can post.

## Hashtags

A hashtag (#) is a keyword or phrase that has a hashtag as a prefix. Here is how it looks: #Himalayan cats. Using a hashtag can increase your chances of being seen on Really Simple Syndication (RSS)[13] feeds.

## Twitter Yellow Pages

If you are looking for someone on Twitter and can't find them, use **twello.com**, the Twitter equivalent of the yellow pages. Here is the link:

**www.twellow.com**

Use Twellow to search for book reviewers on Twitter. Search on "book reviewers."

---

[13] is a family of web feed formats used to publish frequently updated works

## Twitter Steps to Success

Here are some suggestions to get your Twitter account buzzing.

- As your first priority, build a group of followers.
- Make people laugh.
- Link with Amazon.com.
- Link to Web sites that are helpful to writers.
- Tweet about book signings.
- Post links to your **www.goodreads.com** reviews.

## LinkedIn

LinkedIn, also a must-have site for the new writer and/or publisher, is more geared to business than are personal sites like Facebook. It was originally set up to promote individuals to prospective employers and corporations. Over time, it has evolved to a robust and powerful networking site. LinkedIn has many groups that writers can join and participate in.

Even though LinkedIn was created by and for business types who want to promote themselves and their abilities to prospective employers, it is a very effective site to promote your writing business, if used properly.

LinkedIn has three powerful functions that Facebook and Twitter don't currently have:

- You can recommend people and post recommendations for them.
- There is a section where you can post jobs.
- There is a Q&A section where you can ask questions to get expert advice, or answer questions to help establish yourself as the expert.

## Using Social Media

The cardinal rule of social media is: be sociable. Social networking is not commercial, but personal. Facebook is a great place to look for and develop word of mouth recommendations.

If you are going to use Facebook, it works best to also have a blog. WordPress, even the free one at WordPress.com, has a plug-in that can be installed to allow your blog posts link to be posted automatically on to your Facebook page.

To make it easier for people to "friend" you on your blog, put a list of links to your social network accounts on the sidebar of your blog. This makes it easy for people to follow you.

## Specialty Sites for Authors

As a writer in the 21$^{st}$ century, your online presence is the key to success in marketing your book.Those of you who have already written a book know that promoting yourself and your work online can be a convoluted process. You may have a webinar here, a podcast there, your Web site, article postings, blogs and more, spread all over cyberspace. How is a reader to know about all of your online activities?

## Filedby

Wouldn't it be wonderful if there was one place your reader could go to see the various components of your online presence? There is: Filedby.com.

Filedby.com was cofounded by Peter Clifton. Clifton knows the publishing business. He was the former president and CEO of several Ingram Book Group companies.

Clifton's reason for creating Filedby is to "help empower authors and other contributors to represent themselves accurately and market themselves effectively online."

With Filedby, you can tie together all of your profile information and maintain it, all in one place.

| Features | Benefits |
|---|---|
| Search engine optimization | Positively affect the search rank of your author site. |
| Listed in Ingram databases | Your author and book information will automatically be listed in Ingram databases. |
| Promote your book | You can get a pre-publication Web site (fee-based) and promote your book before it is published. |
| Custom outbound links and icons | Link to other sites where you are active. |
| Share videos podcasts, documents and more. | Share all types of media including YouTube, videos, MP3 files and PDFs. |

Some features are fee-based, but most of the features listed above are free.

## Goodreads.com

Goodreads is a privately run "social cataloging" Web site. Started in December 2006, the site lets individuals sign up and register books to create personalized library catalogs and reading lists. Goodreads.com was founded by Otis Chandler, a software engineer and entrepreneur. Members can create their own lists of book suggestions and discussions.

According to some, Goodreads has 2.9 million members and 78 million books titles.

Their goal, according to their Web site, is:

- Get great book recommendations.
- Keep track of what you've read and what you'd like to read.
- Form a book club, answer book trivia, and collect your favorite quotations.

The Goodreads author program is a free service designed to help authors reach their readers. This makes Goodreads a great place to promote your book. As a published author, you can post your profile on Goodreads. Here are some of the things you can do on your profile:

- Add a picture and bio.
- Share list/s of favorite books and your recent reads with your fans.
- Blog and build a band of followers.
- Publicize upcoming events.
- Share book excerpts and other writing.
- Post videos.
- Add the Goodreads author widget to your personal Web site or blog.

Check out the Goodreads Web site and author program at: **www.goodreads.com/author/program.**

 *Self-Publisher's Checklist*

✓ *Set up a fan page on Facebook with the title of your book.*
✓ *Set up a fan page on Facebook for you as an author.*

    ✓  *Set up a LinkedIn profile.*
    ✓  *Open a Twitter account.*
    ✓  *Set up a Filedby account.*
    ✓  *Set up a GoodReads author account.*

*"It's none of their business that you have to learn to write. Let them think you were born that way."*

~Ernest Hemingway

# WHAT YOU WILL LEARN IN THIS CHAPTER

Retail markets, blogging and book fairs

Promotion versus advertising

Indie book awards, podcasting

Press releases, publicity and media

# 18 MARKET WITH IMAGINATION

*"Writing a book is not as tough as it is to haul 35 people around the country and sweat like a horse five nights a week."*

*~Bette Midler*

In this chapter, you will learn to think outside the box. When it comes to self publishing, writing the book is only the first step in the project. As a self-published author, you are the marketing director, CEO, public relations manager, distributor and sales manager, all rolled into one. Don't think in terms of bookstores and online sales only. There are many more places to sell your book. Before we start in earnest, let's take a look at the big picture. As discussed in earlier chapters, the CreateSpace Expanded Channel distribution program can enhance books sales by:

- Listing your book with Baker & Taylor which sell to libraries around the country
- Listing your book with selected retail markets
- Listing your book with Ingram Books as a distributor

## Advertising vs. Promotion

When it comes to book marketing, consider the difference between advertising and promotion. Let's say your book is due to be released in three months and you want to create some buzz and excitement about your book, but your advertising and promotion budget is tight. What do you do? You could place a small ad in one of the literary magazines like *Literary Marketplace* or *Publisher's Weekly*. A tiny ad in these publications will cost you several hundred dollars and may have no effect on sales.

If you had $500 to $1,500 to spend on advertising, what else could you do? My suggestion is that you spend that money on review copies to send to as many qualified people as possible. Send a review copy to the columnists or book reviewer at your local paper. Send a copy to your senator or congressman if the topic is relevant.

Do you belong to a group or association? Send a review copy to the director or president along with a letter letting them know you are available for speaking engagements. Include a color copy of your book cover if you can't afford to send a review copy. Don't be stingy about giving away review copies of your book. Five-hundred dollars' worth of review copies, sent to the right list, can gain you more attention than a well-placed ad in the most prestigious of magazines.

Work on getting book reviews, especially in the first 90 days after your book is released. Most books need to build momentum the first 90 days in order to sustain book purchases over the long haul.

 *Marketer's Note*

*When I was writing my editorial column, I wrote a column about a incident that happened on the field during a Chicago Cubs game. The manager of the Cubs had written a book about his years as a manager and had set up a Google alert for his name. When I mentioned him in my editorial, he saw it through the alert and sent me an autographed copy of his book! He*

*thanked me for mentioning the incident and I in turn mentioned his book in a later column. This is a classic example of how to promote your book rather than advertise it.*

## Promotional Opportunities

One of the best ways to leverage your book is to use it to promote speaking engagements. One of the most lucrative ways to sell books is back-of-room sales (BOR). Many authors who speak at large gatherings make much more money with BOR than they are paid to give the speech or presentation. You can also give your own seminars and make even more money. Sales aren't limited to just your book. You can prepare other materials that relate to your book topic, but are not in your book. These special reports can be sold separately. Authors do it all the time.

## Independent Book Awards

If you feel that your self-published book is good, readable and well edited, think about entering your book in an independent book award contest. Do your homework. Don't just send money to anyone who is hosting a book contest. There are unscrupulous people around; do your research before you enter. I have listed three of the ones that I like below. There are more, and there may be some that are hosted in your state. Most of these contests are backed by organizations and professional writing associations.

### Writer's Digest Self Published-Book Awards

This award has been around for 19 years. Longevity is important when considering which contests are the most credible.The top prize is $3,000, a trip to the Writer's Digest Conference in New York City, Writer's Digest book endorsement, submission to major review houses, and a one-year membership to Publisher's

Marketing Association. Deadlines are generally in April but may change from year to year.

**www.writersdigest.com/competitions**

### The Independent Publisher's Book Award

The Independent Publisher's Book award is 15 years old and was created to honor the best independently published books. Called the IPPY award, it rewards "those who exhibit the courage, innovation, and creativity to bring about change in the world of publishing." IPPY awards are given to publishers of all sizes and budgets, and books are judged with the previously stated criteria in mind. All independent, university, small press, and self publishers who produce books intended for the North American market are eligible to enter. Independent authors using print-on-demand publishing services are welcome to enter their books themselves.

**www.independentpublisher.com**

### Indie Book Awards

The Indie Book Awards is the largest not-for-profit book award program in the country. It is open to independent authors and publishers. The top 60 winners get exposure to 60 agents. Winners participate in a gala reception at the Plaza Hotel in New York City. There are over 60 categories to choose from. Cash prizes run from $500 to $1,500 for first place.

**www.indiebookawards.com**

## Press Release

"Send press releases whenever you have something newsworthy to say, or if you can legitimately link your book, topic or expertise to current news, issues or events," said Susan Lindsey, a 20-year public relations veteran. Don't hesitate to send a press release if the reason for sending it is valid. Sending multiple press releases that aren't newsworthy can irritate and annoy journalists.

 *Marketer's Note*

> *I know a music promoter who was promoting an Elvis tribute concert. Her PR person wrote a press release for her. The concert was held on Halloween. The press release headline said, "Come and Channel the Spirits with Us." It was picked up by the local paper, and ran on the front page of the community section, above the fold! If you can tie your news release to a news event or holiday, it greatly increases the likelihood of media coverage.*

You can track the success of your press release through a site called **www.PRWeb.com.** For a free tutorial on how to write a terrific press release, go to **www.publicityhound.com.** If you are looking for editors, try the Web site U.S. Newspaper List at **www.usnpl.com.** To find radio stations around the world, use **radiolocater.com** or **newslink.org.**

## Podcasts

There are thousands of podcasts on almost any subject. If your book is a niche book, go to iTunes and search on podcasts. Each podcast will come with "show notes." The show notes tell you what the podcast is about. Find several podcasts related to your book topic and make a list. Listen to several of them. If you hear something you think is a good fit, contact the podcaster and tell him you would like to be a guest. If he sounds interested, send him a review copy of your book. Many podcasts have thousands of followers. These listeners are your potential readers.

## Starting a Podcast

If the scope of your book is large enough, you can start your own series of podcasts. With a $200 budget and a computer running Windows 7 or XP, you can start a podcast from your office. You will need at least one microphone (two are better), a pop filter/s, a mixer and software.

Equipment:

- Small analog mixer that can handle two microphones
- Two dynamic microphones  (I have Shure Model C606)
- Two desktop microphone stands
- Two microphone clips
- Two pop filters
- Various adapters, connectors and cables

If you don't plan on interviewing guests, you can start with one microphone, stand and pop filter.

Free Software to download:

- Audacity software[14]
- Levelator
- Lame
- MP3 Tag

Equipment can be purchased from Musicians Friend at **www.musiciansfriend.com** or **www.BSWusa.com**. Information on learning how to podcast can be found at *The Audacity to Podcast* at **www.noodle.mx** or at *Podcast Answer Man* at **www.podcastanswerman.com**.

## Retail Markets

If you are writing a book on dog training, you should approach professional breeders, trainers and groomers. Approach the local pet supply stores and pet grooming shops. If you can strike a deal with the store owner, strive for two things: (1) get them to purchase the books upfront, not on consignment, and (2) a "no-returns"[15] contract. In exchange, give them a 45 percent discount off the list price. This gives the business owner some wiggle room to reduce the book price by 10 percent to their customers and still make a profit.

If you have priced your book properly, you can still make a good profit on book sales. In this way, the book business is the same as any other business; when everyone makes some money, everybody's happy.

---

[14] MAC users will use GarageBand software
[15] Most book stores have a standing return policy which means they can return any unsold books to the publisher or distributor.

## Selling to Indie Book Stores

The self-published and mid-list author's champion is the independent book store. If you don't know it already, big box book stores are not interested in supporting local authors or self-published authors.

Independent bookstore owners are much more likely to carry niche books and books from self-published authors. They are gracious to a fault in supporting local authors, and most are happy to support you if your book is well written and professionally done.

If you have opted for the CreateSpace Expanded Channel, then your book will be available to most book stores, should they decide to order it. I still recommend that you approach independent books stores in your area and offer them a deal to carry your book. An independent book store is an independently owned store. It's usually not part of a chain, but some independents can be quite large with multiple locations.

As a self-published or a traditionally published author, you should be grateful for these brave entrepreneurs. As the big box stores cater to the best sellers, it's the independent books store owners that still believe in the little known writer who may sell fewer than 5,000 or 10,000 books!

As a self-published author, you can talk to them about your book and if you published right, you can make them an offer they can't refuse.

Many indie bookstores have local author sections and are happy to carry your book. Independent bookstores can buy any book through their wholesaler at 40 percent off list price. They will typically give their customer part of this discount—at least 10 percent. That leaves only a 20-30 percent profit margin for the bookstore. You can sweeten the deal for them by offering to sell them your books at a steeper-than-normal discount. You should, in turn, ask for a no-return policy. You may not get it, but try anyway.

You can send the owner a letter with a review copy of your book, but I have found that calling in person is better. Most bookstore owners are gracious and happy to speak with an author in person. Don't be shy. You have produced a quality book, hired a professional editor and book designer, researched the market and know you have a viable book.

Walk in and ask to speak the owner. Say something like this, "Hello, my name is Jim Smith, author of *How to Train your Dog.* Is the owner in?"

If the owner is not available, ask for their phone number and email address and then enter it into your email contact software. It is helpful to categorize these entries as "Bookstore Owners" in your database for later reference. Follow up your visit with an email.

If you are able to speak with the owner, tell them about your book and ask if they have a local author section. This is also a great time to see if they are open to setting up a book signing. I have called on many bookstores and have found the owners to be gracious and receptive to new authors. If your book is well done, it will be well received. Don't waste their time. When you get a chance to speak to the owner, have your 30-second pitch ready!

## Blogging

Once you have a Web site and your book has been released, blogging can be an effective way to promote your book online. Ideally, you would have started your blog about three months before the expected release date. This gives your readers time to know about your book and it gives you time to build curiosity about it online.

*Marketer's Note*

*For business cards and other marketing materials, go to Vista Print at **www.vistaprint.com**. Order business cards that show the front of your book as the background. Be sure to include your email, Web site and name of your book. Sign up for the freebies. Now that you are a published author, you should have business cards, and books with you at all times. Keep a supply of books in the trunk of your car. Most CreateSpace book orders come with the books shrink-wrapped with five to ten books in each bundle. Keep the shrink wrap on until you have to open a packet. It helps protect your book's cover and binding from moisture and damage.*

Running a successful blog is all about the three R's—regularly returning readers! Your job as a successful blogger is to make it as easy as possible for your readers to come back to your blog, again and again. The best and easiest way to do this is through an email subscription service. Only 20 percent of visitors use RSS feeds. Without using an email subscription, you will leave these readers behind.

## FeedBlitz.com

Feedblitz.com is blog-to-email service. FeedBlitz.com will provide you with a script (short block of code) that you can copy and embed on your blog site; this will generate a sign-up box on your blog so that visitors can subscribe to your blog. Once subscribed, they will get an email from your blog with a snippet of your post and a click-through link to your blog.

According to Phil Hollows, CEO of Feedblitz, "If you're not using email, you're missing 80 percent of your potential audience."

## Feedburner.com

Feedburner.com is another blog-to-email service. Make sure when you register with Feedburner that you enable the Pingshot feature. This will increase the likelihood of being discovered by new, potential blog subscribers.

Once you have honed your blogging skills, you may want to consider doing a blog tour. This is nothing more than a virtual book tour that you set up with the writers of some of your favorite blogs.

 *Marketer's Note*

*A friend of mine who knew nothing about blogging or blogging software used Blogger to set up her blog about dogs. Her URL is **http://dawgpause.blogspot.com.** She set the site up in one afternoon. This is a good example of what you can accomplish on your own, learning as you go.*

In today's online, real-time market, traditional book tours may leave something to be desired. A much more affordable and effective way to advertise your book is with a virtual tour. If you are working with a limited budget or traveling is difficult, a virtual tour is your way to reach your readers without leaving the house.

A virtual tour is a win-win for the blogger and the author. Before you can launch your blog tour, you will need to find prospective blogs that are a good fit for your book. There is no definitive directory of blogs where you can go and get a list. But you can search for suitable blogs by using some search tools available online.

## www.blogsearch.google.com

Type in the key search words you are using for your book and see which blogs come up. Remember, you are looking for blogs with heavy traffic that focus on the subject of your book, not on you as the author.

## www.Technorati.com

Technorati is a search tool that monitors traffic on blogs and keeps statistical data. You will need to drill down in Technorati by using the advanced search option to find the most popular blogs that discuss your topic. When Technorati pulls up the blogs, there is a number displayed on the left, and above it, an up or down arrow. The number is how many followers the blog has, and the up or down arrow shows if the blog is trending up or down.

Once you have a working list of 10 to 15 blogs, it's time to prepare the materials that you want to present on the virtual tour. Here is what you will need:

- **Author stats**—Always include your name, book title, price, cover art and author photo
- **Author bio**—This is not a resume, but a writer's statement. If your book is on a technical topic, you will need to include your relevant expertise in your bio.
- **Book description**—The book description tells the visitor what your book is about. You can use the one you wrote for your CreateSpace account.
- **Blurbs**—Blurbs and/or testimonials from your book cover or front matter
- **Book excerpt**—Choose a portion of your book that will leave the reader wanting more. You want the blog host to be excited about having you as a guest.
- **Affiliate link**—Always include the link where visitors can purchase your book. If you sell your book on your own Web site, you should

still use the Amazon link. You will make less money per sale, but you'll have a real chance to improve your Amazon ranking. Ultimately, having a better ranking in Amazon will spur sales and generate attention for your book.

- **Biblio information**—Page count, ISBN, LCCN, binding and publisher.

*Marketer's Note*

*Use Technorati to optimize your blog. You want to make sure that aggregators like Blogline.com and technorati.com are "pinging" your blog. Sign up with both and improve traffic on your blog.*

Once you have gathered your data, have your written material ready and have arranged for dates and times with the blog owners, you simply spend a day, or an afternoon on their blog interacting with their readers.

To learn more about virtual tours, read Steve Weber's book, *Plug Your Book.*

## Book Fairs

Book fairs can be a wonderful market if you have been a smart and savvy self publisher. You will need to have a good price on author copies to make the most profit in this environment. Books sold at book fairs are sold at retail, but the book festival will want their cut—around 30 percent.

If you have never been to a book fair, you need to attend one. Most are huge rooms with tables where piles of books are on display. Each author has a table and will interact with the crowd during the event. Most book fairs are one-day events, but the large ones may go on for days. If your budget is small, start with a one-day event.

Book fairs are a great way to network with other authors. Don't be afraid to mingle and get to know the other exhibitors. Have plenty of business cards to hand out. A desk-top, foam-core stand with the front of your book cover printed on it works great for your tabletop. This will get you attention and you don't see other authors do it often, which means your display will stand out in the crowd.

Most book fairs will have a selection process. You need to contact them early and most will want to carry a book with the current year's copyright. Submitting six months in advance is not too soon to be sure you are included. Many fairs that are held in the fall will have a June cut-off for inclusion.

Choose a fair that has been around for a few years. You also want to pick one that has been advertised widely, has a Web site and is well-known. This will ensure that you will have lots of visitors who may want to buy your book.

A friend of mine went to a book fair recently that had 50 authors there to sell their books, but the event had been poorly advertised and no one came except the authors!

## How Book Fairs Work

Most book fairs establish their own discounts with authors. If you are supplying your self-published book to a book fair via a distributor, then you will be subject to returns. This means that most book fairs will want to return any un-sold books to the distributor, so don't cash your check just yet. Some book fairs will buy books directly from the self-published author.

Once you have chosen your fair, go to the Web site and download the author guidelines. Time is of the essence here, so apply early—several months early, in fact. They will want a sample copy, or two, of your book submitted with the application. To get a partial list of book fairs around the country, try Book TV at **www.booktv.org/Book-Fairs.aspx.**

## Reviews

Every author needs book reviews, but where do you go to get them? There are several sources for review opportunities. The ones you decide to pursue depend on which markets you are after. If you have written a niche book, then sending out thousands of letters and review copies may simply not be practical for you. It is better to locate 50 to 100 people who might take the time to read a review copy of your book and then post it on Amazon.

Because newspapers have cut back so drastically in recent years, getting a book review in a newspaper is harder than ever. But there are other, less traditional ways to get your book reviewed. Try publications that cater to your niche market. A great place to find publications in your niche is *Gale's Directory of Publications and Broadcast Media.* Another great resource for finding television and broadcast names is Gebbie Press. Their Web site is **www.gebbieinc.com.**

You can also contact local columnists. As a former columnist, I can tell you that they are always looking for a column idea and writing a book review may be just what they need. Always send a review copy of your book.

Let's take our Himalayan Cat Lady; where might she send review copies of her book?

- President of the local SPCA
- Local veterinarians
- Pet stores

- Google and Yahoo discussion groups that talk about cat-related subjects
- Amazon Top Reviewers who have reviewed books about animals in general and/or cats in particular

*Marketer's Note*

*Don't pinch budget pennies on review copies. One review copy, in the right person's hands, could mean dozens or hundreds of sales in the long haul. Think of your investment in review copies as advertising, and the best kind of advertising— targeted market advertising!*

## Local Book Reviews

Every author has a local newspaper. If you live in a more cosmopolitan area, you may have a business journal or other magazines that are produced locally. These newspapers, business journals and magazines are often the best place to start to get your first review.

Make a list of all media contacts. Once the list is complete, then pick the top 10 e-zines or newspapers where you would like to get a review. Put together a nice introductory letter using the specific journalist's name and title, enclose a complimentary copy of your book, a one-page spec sheet and a cover letter asking for a review.

When you get a positive review, make copies of it, pull the best quotations and use them for your book's testimonial page or for the back cover. If your book is already in publication, keep trying to get reviews. Don't forget; with the technology of POD, you can always add a new testimonial or a great quotation to your testimonial page or the back cover.

## Kirkus Review

Kirkus Reviews is a paid review site. The cost of getting your book reviewed by Kirkus is $350. CreateSpace and other POD printers offer a Kirkus Review as a part of their promotional package. A paid review is not seen as legitimate by many. I think if you are inventive and resourceful, you can create lots of buzz and some positive reviews without resorting to paying for them, provided you've written a good book.

## Review Resources

Here are some trade publications to which you may want to send a review copy:

*Booklist*
**www.ala.org/booklist/submit.html**

*Library Journal*
**www.libraryjournal.com/info/CA603906.html**

*Publisher's Weekly*
**www.publishersweekly.com/pw/corp/submissionguidelines.html**

James A. Cox, Editor-in-Chief
*Midwest Book Review*
278 Orchard Drive
Oregon, WI  53575-1129
Phone: (608) 835-7937
E-mail: mbr@execpc.com
E-mail: mwbookrevw@aol.com
**www.midwestbookreview.com**

This, by all accounts, is a great company to contact for a book review.

## Amazon Customer Review

Once your book is listed, ask your favorite readers to go to your Amazon page and write a review. Here's how:

Use the search bar in Amazon to find the book.

Click on the book icon.

Scroll down to the bottom of the page to CUSTOMER

REVIEWS, then click on the CREATE YOUR OWN REVIEW button.

Enter the review.

Never ask people who haven't read your book to post a review. The last thing you want is a review that has nothing to do with your book. People who habitually read book reviews to help make their purchase decision will spot it instantly and may be resentful.

Here's the link to find Amazon Top Reviewers:

**www.amazon.com/gp/customer-reviews/top-reviewers.html**

If you want your book to be reviewed by Amazon Top Reviewers, you will need to write them a short, polite letter requesting that they read your book and post a review. Always include a review copy of your book.

Don't ask them to write a positive review, but take your chances and hope they will write a positive review. If you have done your homework and produced a good book with useful content, you should get a good review.

### Self Publisher's Checklist

✓ *Pick a platform for your Web site.*

✓ *Chose 10 blogs that are a good fit for your book and contact the blog owners about doing a blog tour.*

✓ *Write and distribute a press release announcing the coming release of your book.*

✓ *Finish setting up your book in CreateSpace using the Pro Plan and Expanded Channel options.*

✓ *Pick two independent book contests and enter your book in the appropriate category.*

✓ *Set up an Author's Account at Goodreads.com.*

✓ *Create a list of five podcasts that are a good fit with your book topic and email them a review copy and ask if they are interested in having you as a guest.*

✓ *Prepare a one-page book sheet and call on every independent bookstore in your region.*

✓ *Send a copy of your book to James A. Cox at Midwest Book Review.*

# WHAT YOU WILL LEARN FROM THIS CHAPTER

Intellectual capital

Career building

Becoming an expert: speaking

Selling to associations and corporations

# 19 CAREER BUILDING

*"The master in the art of living makes little distinction between his work and his play, his labor and his leisure…his information and his recreation, his love and his religion. He hardly knows which is which. He simply pursues his vision of excellence at whatever he does, leaving others to decide whether he is working or playing. To him he is always doing both."*

~James Michener

Whether you are reading this book because you are already an author thinking about the advantages of self publishing or whether you are writing your first book, you need to understand that writing and publishing your book is only the first step in the process. As a self-published author, your business is your book.

In this chapter, I hope to inspire and encourage you to take it to the next level. Use your book as the foundation on which to build a robust and prosperous business.

## Building Intellectual Capital

Building intellectual capital simply means to increase your knowledge where it's needed. The first area to focus on is technology. Throughout this book, we've seen marketing techniques that leverage technology to increase book sales. Today's authors must be proficient in technology.

Take classes at the library, or through adult education or continuing education programs. You can find great classes on social media, book marketing, Web site building and more. All these skills will help you market and promote your book, and increase your profits.

Lynda.com is an online tutorial Web site that teaches you how to use software such as In Design, Photo Shop, and WordPress. Lynda.com is a subscription site. You pay an annual fee for unlimited use of online tutorials.

Don't be squeamish about spending money on learning. Spending money to learn about technology related to book promotion and publishing is an investment, not an expense! These types of expenditures are tax deductible, and are a vital part of building your credentials as an expert in your field.

## Speaking for Dollars

As an author you have what we call "marketplace credibility." In order to take full advantage of this credibility, you will need to look for opportunities to present your material or to talk about your book. If your book is a non-fiction niche book or a how-to book, then you have information that your readers want and need.

Think about putting together a series of seminars, webinars or other presentations to groups who are interested in your topics. I have given many seminar "overviews" at libraries. Most libraries don't pay unless you are a part of their author series. It is still worth doing even if you don't get paid. Here's why:

- You can sell your books after your presentation.
- You build name recognition.

- You can talk about your paid events during your free event. You can retain mailing list information gathered from attendees.
- You can enhance your reputation and experience as a speaker.

Here are some other venues where you may be able to speak about your book:

- Community clubs like Kiwanis or Rotary Clubs
- Chambers of commerce
- Associations
- Conventions
- Writing conferences

 **_Marketer's Note_**

_Remember, as an author you will be speaking on the subject of your book. That makes you an expert on your topic, so bill yourself as an expert—not a speaker! Ken Blanchard and Spencer Johnson self published "The One Minute Manager." They wanted to be able to sell the book for $15. The experts told them that such a small book would never sell for that much. In three months, they sold 20,000 copies. Eventually they sold the reprint rights—more than 12 million copies have been sold worldwide._

## Writing Articles

As an author you are a wordsmith. Don't confine your writing to your book. There are thousands of magazines on every topic imaginable. Pick several magazines that are in your topic area, and send out queries for articles. The articles can be new material that is related to your book, or even excerpts. Most of these magazines pay fairly well, and they will give you a byline. Always mention your Web site and the name of your book if you have the room. Writing articles online and for magazines, newspapers and other media outlets will help you reach readers who might not otherwise find your book.

## Marketing to Associations

Marketing to associations is one of the most overlooked marketing techniques available. Here's how you do it. At your main library (most branches won't have them), you can search a book called *Gales Encyclopedia of Associations.* There is also an international version of this book.

The book of associations lists every association in America by subject. For each association, there is a contact name, phone number, Web site if applicable, and an email address. The contact name is usually the president or director of the association.

Let's consider the Himalayan cat lady. She might want to know about associations for Himalayan cats, cats, and cat breeding associations. Once you have compiled your list, email the contact names and introduce yourself. Let them know who you are and include a link to your Web site. Tell them you are available for presentations and ask if they would like more information about your book. If they show an interest, send a review copy of the book. (In the front matter of your book, indicate how organizations and associations can order your books in bulk at discounted prices.)

Contacting associations can be time consuming, but effective. This is a great way to build your readers' list and enhance your name and reputation. If you are given the opportunity to speak to a group in your community or elsewhere, post it on your Web site. Use one speaking event to get you into the next one.

### *Marketer's Note*

*Go to: **www.BookTour.com**. Here you can create a free author page for your biography, photo and upcoming tour dates. Your appearances will then be added to BookTour's database and syndicated to a list of book-friendly partner Web sites. BookTour's database can also be searched for venues anywhere in North America.*

## National Speakers Association

The National Speakers Association is a good group to consider joining if you plan to promote your book through presentations. You will learn from the many professional speakers who attend the monthly meetings. The NSA has chapters in most states and large cities. Check their Web site at **http://nsa.org** to find a chapter near you.

If you want a more grassroots approach, join the local Toastmasters group. This is an excellent place to hone the craft of public speaking. Here's their Web site:

**www.toastmasters.org**

## Colleges and Universities

Once you are a published author, you can apply to teach at the local university. If you wrote a memoir, you can teach others about writing a memoir. If your book was a children's book or a book of poetry, then you have an opportunity to teach those things to others.

Approaching an adult education or university continuing learning program director is not as hard as it might seem. I have taught classes for several universities and have approached all of them the same way. I wrote a letter to the program director proposing my course. I outlined the main objectives of the course, and stated why I thought the course would be popular. I also listed the demographics of my potential enrollees.

Here's what you will need to send:

- Your author bio
- Course outline
- A list of reasons why you think the course would be popular
- The main teaching objectives of the course
- Your target market demographics

## Selling to Corporations

Depending on the subject of your book, it may be wise to offer it to corporations. Most people don't realize it, but hundreds of thousands of books are purchased by corporations every year. Why? They give them to customers as premiums, or pass them out to salespeople and/or employees as incentives or educational aides.

### Marketer's Note

*A doctor wrote a book on how to market a clinical practice. He tried to promote it, but was largely unsuccessful at selling his book through traditional outlets. Eventually he tried selling his book to pharmacies to use as a giveaway item for the doctors that they called on. There are strict rules on what pharmacies can give away as incentives to doctors, but educational products like books are OK. He found a drug company that was interested and they ended up buying over 120,000 books.*

### Self Publisher's Checklist

- ✓ *Take a class on book marketing and promotion through a continuing education program at an adult education center or university.*
- ✓ *Call a local library branch and ask about setting up a presentation on your topic or a reading.*
- ✓ *Write a 600-word article on a topic related to your book. Write and send a query letter to a magazine editor, on spec for publication.*
- ✓ *Attend a Toastmasters group meeting or a local chapter meeting of the National Speakers Association.*

# WHAT YOU WILL LEARN IN THIS CHAPTER

The big plan

Time tracking
and building a
publisher's

calendar

Taking it to the
next level

Branding

# 20 PUT IT ALL TOGETHER

*"Be obscure clearly."* ~*E.B. White*

## The Master Plan

As a self-published author, you have an opportunity to create your own marketing plan, on your own schedule. This is both a privilege and a peril. Because you won't have a traditional publisher looking over your shoulder, it's important that you have a plan.

If you were planning a garden or a trip, you would have specific goals in mind and a plan of action; writing and marketing your self-published book is no different.

## The Publisher's Calendar

As an author, whether you are traditionally published, or self published, you need a detailed plan. Things often take longer than you anticipate, so give yourself some wiggle room in your publication schedule. My advice is to figure out your target publication date, then add three months.

Once the publication calendar is finished, mark off each task as it is accomplished. The first time you may not anticipate everything that needs to be done. That's OK; be flexible and work with what you can do. It will help you to use the self publisher's checklists, found at the end of each chapter. These task lists are the foundation of a publisher's calendar. You just need to add your target completion dates.

## Branding

Dan Blank wrote a book about branding called, *Branding Yourself.* In his book, he talks a lot about standing out. How can we, as authors, differentiate ourselves and our work?

As an author, you will need to connect to your reader—not just with your book, but with your story as well. What is your back story? How did you come to be a writer? Some of your back story should come from your *About the Author* page in your book. Some of it should come from presentations, book signings and speeches.

Your brand should be clear and concise so that it can be easily communicated to your readers. Branding is not just about giving the facts, but rather, it's about your passion, your emotions.

Here are some things to work on to solidify your brand:

- Be able to give a 30- to 90-second elevator speech about your book.
- Know your back story, and be able to tell someone how you came to be a writer, and to write your book. Again, use clear and concise language, but with an emotional or humorous edge.
- Know what makes your book unique.
- Know your "tag line" or sub-title and be able to roll it off your tongue at a moment's notice.

## Summary

Now that your book is written and the promotion has begun in earnest, you will need to keep books with you at all times. Tell everyone you know about your book. Talk about your book on your social network sites, at parties or at business functions.

There are more ways to market your book and more groups to market to than you realize. Take the time to sit down and see if you can come up with a list of 100 non-traditional outlets where you could sell your book. Here a few to get you started:

### Groups and Specialty Stores

| | |
|---|---|
| Kinkos | Book clubs |
| Grocery chains | Veterinarians |
| Kmart | Sewing groups |
| WalMart | Writing groups |
| Target | Chiropractors |
| Airport gift shops | Hobby stores |
| Libraries | Museum store |
| Home schoolers | State parks |
| Associations | Historic houses |
| Politicians | Artist groups |
| Chambers of commerce | Women's clubs |
| U.S. Chamber of Commerce | Business groups |
| Life coaches | Salespeople |
| Doctors' offices | Dentist offices |
| Pediatrician offices | Floral shops |
| eBay | Network marketing companies |

Keep promoting and *keep on keeping on.*

# BIBLIOGRAPHY

*Aiming at Amazon:* Shepherd (ISBN 978-0-938497-43-1)
Shepherd Publication

*Branding Yourself:* Deckers (ISBN 978-0-7897-4727-3)
Pearson Education, Inc.

*Damn, Why Didn't I Write That?:* McCutcheon (ISBN 1-885956-55-6)
Quill Driver Books

*Dan Poynter's Self Publishing Manual:* Poynter (ISBN 978-1-56860-134-2)
Para Publishing

*Guerilla Marketing for Writers:* Levinson, Frishman, Larsen, Hancock
(ISBN 978-1-60037-660-3)
Morgan-James

*Plug Your Book:* Weber (ISBN 978-0-9772406-1-6)
Weber Books

*The Complete Idiot's Guide to Self Publishing:* Sander (ISBN 1-59257-358-5)
Alpha Books

*The 4-Hour Workweek:* Ferriss (978-0-307-46535-1)
Crown Publishing Group

*The Long Tail: Why the Future of Business Is Selling Less of More*: Anderson
(ISBN 978-1-4013-0966-4)
Hyperion

*Tribes:* Godin (ISBN 978-1-59184-233-0)
Penquin Group

# APPENDIX A

## WRITING and PROFESSIONAL GROUPS

The Authors Guild
31 East 32nd Street, 7th Floor
New York, NY 10016
Phone: (212) 563-5904
Fax: (212) 564-5363
Email:staff@authorsguild.org
www.authorsguild.org

Mystery Writers of America
1140 Broadway, Suite 1507
New York NY 10001
Phone: (212) 888-8171
Fax: (212) 888-8107
www.mysterywriters.org

Society of Children's Book Writers & Illustrators
8271 Beverly Blvd.
Los Angeles, CA 90048
Phone: (323) 782-1010 (9 a.m. to 5:30 p.m., Pacific time)
Fax: (323) 782-1892
Email: scbwi@scbwi.org
www.scbwi.org

American Society of Journalists and Authors
1501 Broadway, Suite 403, New York, NY 10036
Phone: (212) 997-0947
Fax: (212) 937-2315
www.asja.org

Romance Writers of America
14615 Benfer Rd.
Houston, TX 77069
Phone: (832) 717-5201
Email: info@rwa.org
www.rwa.org/cs/home

**LIBRARY**

American Library Association (ALA)

Public Library Association—Contains information regarding continuing education, awards and grants, publications, and resources on the Web.
Manager of Publications
Kathleen M. Hughes[16]
ext. 4028
khughes@ala.org

The Independent Book Publishers Association—The largest non-profit trade association representing independent publishers of books, audio, video and CDs. This group sponsors the Book Expo America and American Library Association's Show.

www.ibpa-online.org

---

[16] Serves as editor of *Public Libraries* magazine, manages PLA publications program, PLA blog, and Public Library Data Service Statistical Report project.

## BOOK EDITORS

Susan E. Lindsey
Savvy Communication LLC
P.O. Box 6746
Louisville, Kentucky 40206-0746
Phone: (502) 585-2419 or (502) 415-1863
Email: Info@savvy-comm.com
www.Savvy-comm.com

## REVIEWERS & PUBLISHERS' MAGAZINES

Amazon.com
Attn. Editorial – [Product & Category]
701 Fifth Avenue
Suite 1500
Seattle, WA 98104

ALA Booklist
American Library Association
http://ala.org

*Choice Magazine*
www.als.org/arcl/choice/home.html

*Canadian Author*
Canadian Authors Association
www.canauthors.org

Kirkus Reviews
www.kirkusreviews.com/kirkusreveiwes/indes.jsp

*Library Journal*
www.libraryjournal.com

*Publishers Weekly*
www.publishersweekly.com
*School Library Journal*
www.SchoolLibraryJournal.com

*Writer's Digest*
http://writersdigest.com

# APPENDIX B

## Recommended Reading

*1001 Ways to Market Your Book*
By John Kremer

*Aiming at Amazon*
By Aaron Shepherd

*Branding Yourself*
By Lacey Deckers

*Damn! Why didn't I write that?*
by Marc McCutcheon

*Guerilla Marketing for Writers*
By Levinson, Frishman, Larsen, Hancock

*No More Mondays*
By Dan Miller

*Plug Your Book*
By Steve Weber

*Teach Yourself WordPress in 10 Minutes*
*By* Tomasi and Steppe

*The Complete Idiot's Guide to Self Publishing*
By Jennifer Basye Sander

*The 4-Hour Workweek*

By Timothy Ferriss

*The Purple Cow*
By Seth Godin

*The Self Publishing Manual: How to Write, Print & Sell Your Own Book*
By Dan Poynter

*The Writer's Market, Deluxe Edition*
Writer's Digest Books

*Tribes*
By Seth Godin

*Unleashing the Idea Virus*
By Seth Godin

"I think I did pretty well, considering I started out with nothing but a bunch of blank paper."

~Steve Martin

INDEX

Adobe Acrobat .............................. 121
Adobe In Design CS5 ..................... 92
affiliate marketing ....................... 185
Amazon Associate ........................ 185
Amazon Bestsellers Rank History
........................................... 179
Amazon Editorial Review ......... 182
Amazon Encore ......................... 4, 186
Appendices ..... 39, 55, 56, 106, 151
Application to Participate .... 80, 81, 82
artist's statement ........................... 40
Assigning an ISBN ...................... 140
author copies ..... 6, 18, 20, 72, 134, 148, 153, 157, 158, 159, 233
Author Profile ...................... 157, 177
Author's Central account 176, 179
author's platform. .......................... 25
aWeber ............................................ 212
Back matter ..................................... 38
Baker & Taylor 143, 189, 192, 194, 195, 221
banner .............................................. 150
Barcode ....................... 115, 117, 191
Bibliography .................................... 55
BISAC category .................... 127, 149
blog tour ............................... 231, 239
Blogger ............................................ 199
blogging .............. 200, 201, 229, 231
Bluebeam PDF Revu ............ 54, 122
blurb .................................. 36, 51, 113
blurbs ...... 19, 36, 38, 116, 118, 193
Book fairs ............................. 233, 234
Book Industry Study Group .... 127, 149
book jacket .................................... 127
book reviews ....... 19, 222, 235, 238

Book Title Form ............................... 76
Books In Print ... 75, 76, 77, 86, 140, 141
BookScan. ...................................... 179
BOR sales ...................................... 223
Bowker. 74, 75, 76, 77, 79, 87, 140, 141
Branding ........................................ 250
Cataloging in Publication Division
........................................... 85
Chicago Manuel of Style ................ 47
Choice .............................................. 193
CIP ..................................... 83, 84, 190
Contact the Author page .............. 34
copyright 35, 59, 60, 61, 62, 64, 66, 68, 80, 83, 84, 85, 135, 143, 190, 193, 234
Copyright iv, 35, 59, 60, 61, 62, 64, 65, 66, 67, 68, 85, 191
Copyright Clearance Center ........ 66
Copyright page ................................ 35
cover design ... 19, 20, 22, 109, 111, 117, 126, 128, 149
CreateSpace ..... 5, 8, 11, 18, 19, 20, 21, 22, 53, 54, 68, 71, 72, 73, 74, 75, 76, 79, 83, 85, 86, 91, 92, 98, 99, 107, 109, 112, 113, 121, 122, 125, 127, 128, 129, 130, 131, 132, 133, 134, 136, 138, 139, 140, 141, 142, 143, 144, 146, 147, 148, 149, 150, 151, 152, 153, 154, 171, 176, 178, 179, 181, 186, 194, 195, 205, 221, 228, 230, 232, 239
eBook .............................. 75, 92, 140
embedded video .......................... 207
Epilogue ........................................... 39
eStore ...................................... 197, 204

Expanded Distribution Channel
............................... 150, 179, 195
Facebook....26, 202, 209, 210, 211,
212, 214, 215, 217, 275
Facebook Markup Language.... 212
Fair Use...............................................63
FBML.................................................. 212
Federation of Reproduction
Rights Organizations ...............67
Filedby ......................... 215, 216, 218
first draft............................ 45, 46, 47
Footers................................... 103, 104
Foreword.................................35, 37
front matter 35, 38, 102, 104, 232,
244
Gales Encyclopedia of
Associations.................................28
Global settings ...............................99
glossary ..............................................39
GoDaddy...........................................201
Golden Rules for Authors...........158
Goodreads ................... 216, 217, 239
Google pages....................................200
gutter....................... 94, 99, 100, 102
Headers.............................. 103, 104
IFRRO ...............................................67
imprint name ....................... 140, 141
Independent Publisher's Book
award ........................................ 224
Independent self-publishing.......20
Indie Book Awards ...................... 224
Ingram Books......20, 194, 195, 221
intellectual capital......................... 241
interior layout.... 17, 19, 20, 22, 53,
54, 72, 91, 92, 93, 103, 143, 144
Introduction ..................... 35, 37, 38

ISBN..22, 35, 56, 71, 72, 73, 74, 75,
76, 79, 80, 83, 85, 86, 114, 117,
125, 136, 139, 140, 141, 146,
154, 191, 193, 233
Kindle ..................................... 178, 186
*Kirkus Reviews*............. 190, 193, 237
LCCNiv, xxiv, 35, 71, 72, 73, 79, 80,
82, 142, 143, 154, 191, 193, 233
*Library Journal*. 190, 193, 194, 237
Library of Congress Number ......79
Library Reviews ........................... 193
Lightning Source..............................20
LinkedIn ...................... 202, 214, 218
Listmania ....................................... *185*
*Literary Journal* ...............................28
LLC..........................................73, 74, 79
LOC .......................79, 80, 82, 83, 142
Lynda.com ...................................... 242
media kit ............ 160, 161, 163, 172
*Member Dashboard* ............ 132, 134
mid-list author......................25, 228
myidentifiers.com ....................... 141
National Speakers Association 245
ndex.......................................................39
niche books ...................................... 8
Partnered self-publishing ............19
PCN...................................... 80, 85, 136
PDF ...... ...54, 55, 56, 121, 122, 123,
143, 144, 151, 152, 206, 216
PDF file...54, 55, 121, 122, 123,
151, 206
POD...... 3, 4, 5, 7, 12, 18, 19, 20, 21,
22, 23, 31, 39, 50, 74, 75, 79, 84,
95, 98, 158, 159, 236, 237, 273
podcast......162, 172, 215, 226, 227
Preface ............................................37
press release.....162, 164, 225, 239

Primo PDF ............................. 55

print-on-demand ........*3, 55, 74, 112,*
*138, 224, 273*

Pro Package ................................. 153

Pro Plan 22, 72, 150, 153, 195, 239

proof ................... 142, 144, 151, 152

Publisher of Record ........................ 75

Publisher's Weekly .......25, 28, 190,
193, 194, 222, 237

Quality Books ........84, 86, 189, 190,
192, 194, 195

ranking .... 147, 175, 179, 180, 204,
233

registration ......................................... 64

Reproductive Rights Organization
................................................. 66

review iv, xvi, 15, 72, 95, 115, 133,
142, 182, 183, 184, 186, 187,
193, 222, 223, 226, 229, 235,
236, 237, 238, 239, 244

Right justified ................................. 102

RRO ............................................... 66

search algorithm ............................. 41

search words ......41, 112, 125, 126,
136, 147, 232

second draft ........................ 46, 47, 48

self-publish .v, 3, 5, 7, 8, 16, 19, 50,
54, 112, 273, 274

Selling Paragraph ......................... 115

Serif fonts ............................................ 94

social media .................................... 209

spine .......... 110, 111, 118, 144, 191

standard trim sizes ...............98, 138

sub-title ........ 41, 42, 112, 118, 128,
135, 136, 154, 250

symbol © ........................................... 62

Table of Contents ........37, 103, 106,
113, 151, 191

tag ................79, 122, 126, 181, 250

Tagging ............................................. 181

Technorati ...................................... 232

template .....92, 109, 143, 144, 200,
201, 202

*The Elements of Style* ....................... 47

*The Purple Cow* .............................. 203

TinyURL ............................................ 213

Top Reviewer ................................ 183

Top Reviewers. 183, 184, 236, 238

traditional publishers .. 6, 7, 10, 11,
16, 20

trim size ....................................97, 138

Twitter ......xxv, 202, 210, 212, 213,
214, 218

vanity press .................................18, 19

Weebly.com ......................... 201, 206

Word Press ....... 200, 201, 202, 206,
242, 257

World Cat .............................................86

# GLOSSARY

**afterword**—A final concluding section to a book, written by the author

**Adobe InDesign**—Desktop publishing software application by Adobe™

**ALA**—American Library Association

**Amazon Associates**—Affiliate arm of Amazon where Web site owners can sell books on Amazon for a commission

**Amazon Central**—Central author account for authors who have books for sale on Amazon

**Amazon Breakthrough Novel Award**—Annual award for the best novel self-published through CreateSpace

**Amazon Editorial Review**—A book review by the Amazon editorial board

**Amazon Encore**—Amazon's imprint that specializes in promoting and marketing books that are self published and have been overlooked by customers

**American Library Association**—Largest library association in the US

**ancillary pages**—Extra pages

**appendices**—Special interest pages in the back matter of a book which give readers extra information

**author bio**—A writer's statement that tells the reader how and why the writer came to write the book

**author platform**—A group of people that the author hopes to have some influence with as potential readers/buyers of the author's books

**Autocrit**—An automated editing program that is fee based

**BISAC**—Book Industry Systems Advisory Committee; a committee of the Book Industry Study Group (BISG).

**Baker & Taylor**—North American book distributor

**barcode**—A digitized, magnetic code that contains digitized information that can be read by a barcode scanning device; book barcodes are called BookLan EANs

**Blogger**—Blogging platform software by Google

**Bluebeam PDF Revu**—Word-to-PDF file conversion program

**blurb**—A promotional announcement or book testimonial

**book fair**—Conference where authors sell their books to the general public

**book price**—List price of a book

**BOR**—Back-of-room sales

**Branding**—To develop a recognizable identity in the marketplace for a person or product

**BTIC**—Butt time in chair

**cataloguing-in-publication (CIP)**—bibliographic information supplied by the Library of Congress, printed on the copyright page.

**Copyediting**—Checking a manuscript for grammar, punctuation, spelling and usage

**copyright**—The exclusive right to make copies, license, and otherwise exploit a literary, musical or artistic work

**copyright notice**—Physical designation of copyright on a literary work, music, art or CD. Usually displayed as "© copyright *copyright-holders-name.*"

**copyright registration**—The process of sending notification and a deposit of a literary, musical or other work to the copyright office of the U.S. government

**Copyright Clearance Center**—Central clearing house in the U.S. for authors to register their work in order to receive royalty payments from foreign countries

**CreateSpace** —A print-on-demand (POD) publisher and division of Amazon.com

**Dedication**—A sentence or two, to a page, in the front matter of a book that pays tribute to individuals or groups

**design credit**—Listing of a graphic designer's name on the back cover or on the copyright page of a book

**distributor**—A company that represents an author's book to another entity or entities such as libraries or bookstores. Distributors have a traveling sales force and sell individual books to wholesalers, libraries, and retail outlets.

**e-book**—An electronic version of a book that can be stored on an e-reader, mobile phone or downloaded to a computer in a PDF format

**editing**—The act of reading a body of text for the purpose of correcting errors in spelling, grammar or usage, as well as checking for clarity, chronology, coherency, consistency and correctness.

**EIN**—Employer Identification Number, issued by the federal government to business entities

**epilogue**—Part of the back matter, the epilogue is a page or series of pages of writing that brings the reader up to date on characters and matters contained in the book

**Expanded Distribution Channel**—CreateSpace program for self-published authors that incorporates the author's book into the distribution cycles of Ingram Books and Baker & Taylor

**e-zine**—An electronic newsletter or magazine

**Fair Use**—The use of a limited amount of copyrighted material without getting permission

**Facebook**—Social networking site

**FBML**—Facebook Markup Language

**Filedby**—Author Web site specializing in helping authors consolidate a listing of all of their online marketing: Web site, books, events and activities

**footers**—Line or lines at the bottom of a printed page that may contain page numbers or other information

**front matter**—All the pages of a book that appear before the main text

**fulfillment**—The process of fulfilling orders, including picking orders, packing and shipping

**galleys**—Pre-publication copies of a book sent to potential reviewers. Galleys can be photocopies of the book with the pages cut to the size of the published book.

**godaddy.com**—A Web site with templates that can be used to create other Web sites in a short period of time

**Goodreads**—A specialized Web site featuring reading lists and lists of favorite books by readers all around the world

**gutter**—The blank or white space between text on two facing pages of a book

**hardcover**—A book that is bound in boards

**headers**—One or two lines at the top of the pages of a book listing the page number, and/or other information

**HTML**—Hyper text markup language used to create the look and feel of a Web site

**imprint**—The name under which a publishers prints a line of books. Publishers may have several imprints.

**Independent publishing**—A self-published author using a POD printer for printing only and performing all other publishing functions himself or contracting them out

**Ingram Books**—The largest book distributor in the U.S.

**Intellectual capital**—The knowledge base of an individual that can be used to generate income

**Interior layout**—The inside layout of the text and graphics of a book

**International Standard Book Number (ISBN)**—International Standard Business Number issued by Bowker.com in the U.S. to help track online and retail sales of books.

**Justify**—Aligning text on a page that in a manner that results in even margins on both sides

**Kirkus Reviews**—Book reviewer

**landing page**—A one-page, static Web page used primarily for advertising a specific product or service

**LCCN**—Library of Congress Control Number used to identify a literary, artistic or musical work

**LCN**—Aka LCCN

**Leading**—Spacing between lines in a text document (pronounced "ledding")

*Library Journal*—A library trade magazine specializing in book reviews and articles of interest to librarians

**Library of Congress**—National library of the U.S.

**Lightning Source**—The POD printing division of Ingram Books

**LinkedIn**—Social networking site for professionals seeking employment and networking with other professionals

**Listmania**—A list-building application on Amazon.com that allows readers to build lists of favorite books to be shared with other readers

*Literary Marketplace*—The book publishing industry directory

**media**—Communications formats that reach broad audiences; traditional media outlets include newspapers, magazines, television and radio.

**media kit**—A comprehensive collection of information about an author and his/her books which is used primarily by the media

**orphans**—Widows and orphans are words or short lines at the beginning or end of a paragraph, which are left dangling at the top or bottom of a column, separated from the rest of the paragraph.

**partnered self publishing**—A form of self publishing where the author chooses services provided by the POD on an a la carte basis

**PCN** (Pre-assigned Control Number)—The term the Library of Congress uses for the number assigned to a title before publication

**PDF**—Portable Document Format produced and developed by Adobe

**perfect bound book**—Consist of various sections with a cover made from heavier paper, glued together at the spine with a strong flexible glue.

**plagiarism**—Copying the work of another author and passing it off as one's own work

**POD**—Print-on-demand, a technology that combines the use of a high-speed digital printer with a high-speed book binder that, together, can print and bind perfect bound books in seconds

**podcasting**—A podcast is a series of digital media files (either audio or video) that are released episodically and often downloaded through Web sites or iTunes

**preface**—An introduction to a book written by the author of the book

**Pre-assigned Control Number**—See PCN

**pre-publication file**—A Word or text file that has been converted to a PDF to be uploaded to a POD

**press release**—An announcement distributed to media outlets (also called a news release or media release)

**print-on-demand (POD)**—Publishers who use high-speed, digital printers and binders to produce perfect bound books quickly. These books can then be purchased one at a time as needed.

**Pro Plan**—CreateSpace Pro Plan allows authors to purchase author copies of their books at a discounted price

**Proof**—A pre-publication duplicate of your soon-to-be printed book

**Publisher of record**—The entity who purchased the ISBN from Bowker is listed as the publisher of record in the *Forthcoming Books In Print* and *Books In Print* databases

**Quality Books**—A distributor of books, working primarily with libraries in the U.S.

**ranking**—Amazon's method of comparing each book sale on their site to every other book sale on their site and assigning a numeric value to each book based on that data

**recto**—Right page of a book

**sans serif**—A typeface in which characters have no serifs

**section breaks**—A Word function that separates one document into separately formatted sections

**serif**—An embellishment on the main strokes of a typeface character

**substantive editing**—Also called content editing, substantive editing means making sure that a document is well-organized and clearly written.

**tags**—A non-hierarchical key word or term assigned to a piece of information

**template**—An electronic document with preset margins, typography, and/or artwork

**top reviewers**—An Amazon designation for book reviewers who have reviewed the most books on Amazon while getting the most positive ratings of those reviews from other readers

**Trim size**—The finished size of a book after the signatures have been trimmed and folded

**Twitter**—A social networking and micro-blogging service that enables its users to send and read messages known as tweets

**vanity press**—A subsidy press

**verso**—Left page of a book

**widow**—Widows and orphans are words or short lines at the beginning or end of a paragraph, which are left dangling at the top or bottom of a column, separated from the rest of the paragraph.

**WordPress**—Dynamic open source publishing tool for managing Web site content using a web browser

# ABOUT THE AUTHOR

I was born in Missouri, in the tiny town of Poplar Bluff. As a young child I moved with my family to Louisville. Riding bikes (road and mountain bikes), was my passion for many years. At one point, I rode 150 miles per week—I had a resting heart rate of 56 and the legs to prove it. Writing was never a part of my life plan. I came to it in small steps—a business woman first, a writer second.

After a short career in banking, I went back to college for a computer science degree and opened a computer network design company. I left the computer business after 13 years and found myself writing copy for brochures, developing PowerPoint presentations and writing employee manuals for other businesses. It seemed to me that the two consistent things in the many iterations of my career were computers and writing. In 2008, I began writing seriously with a political column called *Thoughts from the Hungry Side of Daybreak*.

In 2009, I became director of Women Who Write, Inc., a nonprofit formed in Louisville, Kentucky in 1992. In December of 2009, I won first place for a narrative non-fiction piece called *Banking on an Angel* which was published in *OnAngels* print magazine and online. I have also had several poems published in various anthologies.

As director of Women Who Write, Inc., I led the group in self publishing their 16th anthology using POD (print-on-demand) technology, a first for our group. I went on to self publish two more books for this group, in addition to *Self Publishing for Virgins*.

I am a speaker on the topic of self publishing, book promotion, and e-books. I conduct workshops on how to self publish at universities and other venues and am a frequent guest at writer's conferences such as the Kentucky Women's Book Festival, American Society of University Women, Duckon, Fandom Fest and others.

I love the opportunity that self publishing provides to all writers. I am passionate about making sure that the creator of the work, the author, is paid for their time, creativity, and dedication to their published book. Self publishing is a great way to accomplish that worthy goal.

Writing books that move people forward,

Peggy Barnes DeKay

http://selfpublishingforvirgins.com
http://peggydekay.com

# FORTHCOMING BOOKS

**E-Books for Virgins**

**Stealth Marketing for Authors**

---

[i] Statistical data form Facebook website http://www.facebook.com/press/info.php?statistics

Made in the USA
Charleston, SC
10 June 2011